Reading

Colossians and Philemon

Over a Glass

of Turkish Tea

John A. Forrester

Reading Colossians and Philemon Over a Glass of Turkish Tea

John A. Forrester

Pastors Attic Press

www.pastorsatticpress.com

Reading Colossians and Philemon Over a Glass of Turkish Tea Copyright © 2015 by John A. Forrester. All rights reserved.

Scripture quotations are from The Holy Bible, English Standard Version, copyright © 2001 by Crossway Bibles, a division of Good News Publishers. Used by permission. All rights reserved.

For

my dear children and grandchildren

and a few other good friends

who might be interested

in such a devotional

pilgrimage

Contents

Introduction	9
1. On the Road Again	12
All Gift—All Grace (Col. 1:1)	
2. Arrival	16
Saints Unmerited (Col. 1:2a)	
3. On the Train	22
Through Grace, To Shalom (Col. 1:2b)	
4. At Home In Denizli	29
Thank You Lord (Col. 1:3-6)	
5. A Visit To Old Colossae	33
A Ministry of Encouragement (Col. 1:7-8)	
6. And a Visit to Laodicea	38
Tending the Garden (Col. 1:9-12)	
7. On the Eve Of Sacrifice	46
Ransomed, Healed, Restored, Forgiven (Col.1:13-14)	
8. A Divine Appointment	51
Very God Of Very God (Col. 1:15-20)	
9. Another Divine Appointment	57
Safely Home—Whole and Holy (Col. 1:21-23)	
10. Sunday Worship In Denizli	60
Four-Wheel-Drive Prayers (Col. 1:24-2:3)	

11. Over Lunch 65
    Inoculate Us Against Delusion (Col. 2:4-13)
12. Next Stop, Adana 70
    Dept Free!—Dept Free! (Col. 2:13-14)
13. Visiting a Dear Friend 75
    Devils Declawed (Col. 2:15)
14. Tuesday 82
    Shame-Proofing the Church (Col. 2:16-23)
15. Of Soles and Souls 90
    Radical Reorientation (Col. 3:1-4)
16. Language Drills 97
    Off With the Old (Col. 3:5-11)
17. Oranges Off the Tree 103
    From Rags To Righteousness! (Col. 3:12-14)
18. No Men Allowed 109
    He Sets the Solitary In Families (Col. 3:15-17)
19. The Turkish Face Of Jesus 112
    Where the Rubber Meets the Road (Col. 3:18-4:1)
20. North To the Black Sea 120
    Two Salty Conversations (Col. 4:2-6)
21. Chestnuts Roasting 128
    In the Image Of Our Relational God (Col. 4:7-18)
22. Fish and Cats 134
    Philemon's Laundry—For All To See! (Phlm. 1-3)
23. Historic Faith 139
    Recipe For True Spirituality (Phlm. 4-7)
24. Searching For Lost Sheep 146
    Equal In Christ (Phlm. 8-22)
25. Last Goodbyes 151
    Amazing Grace (Phlm. 23-25)

Introduction

In the fall of 2014 Betty and I spent three weeks traveling across Turkey. Some years earlier we had lived in that country for almost three years and had come to love the land and its people. This was our third return visit and, we pray, not the last.

Turkey is often called the "Other Holy Land" because of its deep connection to the Bible. The Tigris and Euphrates rivers of the Eden story originate in Turkey. Noah's Mount Ararat, and Abraham's Haran, are also there. Solomon traded horses with the Hittites whose capital was near modern Ankara.

And the land plays a central role in the New Testament, so much of which was written either to or from Turkey. Christians were first called Christians in Antioch, in south-east Turkey. The apostle Paul was born in Tarsus, just three hours west of there. And, of course, Paul did much of his missionary work across western Turkey. The famous seven churches of Revelation were clustered in the south-west. Later, Constantinople (Istanbul today), would be at the center of the Christian world for a thousand years. The Hagia Sophia church building, still standing after 1400 years, is a magnificent reminder of that remarkable era.

So we enjoy this land for its biblical connections, for its rich history and geography, for its role as a cultural bridge between east and west, but especially for its warm and hospitable people, some of whom, both Muslim and Christian, have become like family to us.

An important part of this trip was our extended stay in the modern city of Denizli. We wanted to meet the small group of believers hidden there (like yeast!) among the half-million inhabitants. And since Denizli is quite close to the site of ancient Colossae, Paul's letters to that church provide an appropriate meditative backdrop to our trip. How moving it is to revisit the site of that once important city, wandering through the archaeological rubble, wondering where Epaphras, the founding father of that church, might have lived. Or musing about Philemon and Onesimus whose complex relationship we learn about in Paul's letter to Philemon.

So along with this journal I have included meditations and prayers on passages from these two New Testament letters, Colossians and Philemon. For some readers this little book might work as a daily devotional reading. Take your time, savour the journey, six days a week for a month would work well. Make notes of your own reflections, write out your own prayers as prompted by the verses of the day. Allow the Word of God to sink deep.

On the devotional page I have included only a few words of the daily reading. The whole passage for the day is indicated in the top left-hand corner. I encourage you to have your Bible in hand and read the entire selection. All Scripture quotations here are from the English Standard Version, but why not read other translations alongside? These two letters carry us to the heart of the Gospel, which means, of course, to the heart of Jesus. Have a blessed journey!

From Denizli we traveled further east, to Adana. We lived in this city for a year and a half. So we know the place well and have dear friends there. Then an overnight train and an intercity bus took us to the Black Sea coast for a memorable stay with more close friends. We topped off our pilgrimage with a few days in magnificent Istanbul.

No, this is not high adventure with big-name people. We didn't get to meet the prime minister! No crowds followed us, certainly no press. This is an ordinary tale of ordinary people. Yet, perhaps, it is the very ordinariness of our tale that makes it print-worthy. The world is full of normal, average, everyday people. Yet over all this ordinariness, is the near presence of our extraordinary God—Father, Son, and Holy Spirit, busy with his extraordinary work. There may be times when faith dwells on the mountaintop. But most of the time faith dwells along the side-streets of this world, in kitchens and offices, as ordinary people discover the unseen Almighty One, and begin the greatest of all pilgrimages, the life of faith.

If this little book encourages you to remember Turkey in your prayers, and perhaps even spend some time there yourself, it will have been well worth the effort of writing. If this book leads you closer to the heart of God we will be more than pleased.

Because this account is going to print I have changed names and disguised one or two incidents to protect the privacy of people involved.

Now open your Bible, pour yourself a glass of Turkish tea, and enjoy the journey.

1. On the Road Again

On a late September Friday morning we drive out of Merritt up onto the infamous Coquihalla highway (a.k.a. "The Highway Through Hell!" of TV fame) and head for the coast. But this time of year there is no sign of snow, even at the summit. It turns out to be more like heaven than that other place. We relax and enjoy the spectacular scenery of the BC coastal ranges. We plan to spend three nights with our family in Vancouver before setting out on our latest expedition. This gives us time to visit friends and celebrate family birthdays.

Sunday morning at our former church is, as Betty says, like coming home. What a vibrant, international throng! There are so many old friends eager to greet us and talk. But there are lots of changes too. It is ten years since we left and many of our old friends have "graduated" from this earth. Happily there are lots of new faces also in this thriving congregation. Yes, we have many homes in this world (PEI, Vancouver, Turkey, Etobicoke, Merritt, the Netherlands.) But of course, as someone graciously reminds me after the worship service, our true home is with the Lord.

Then, early Monday morning, our son kindly trundles his aging parents off to the beautiful Vancouver airport for the start of their latest adventure. Our flight is scheduled for 9:10 but we set out extra early because there is a question mark hanging over our tickets. For some reason Air Canada will not let us check in online in the usual 24-hour window prior to take off. We pray about this the night before and sleep reasonably well. I wonder if our convoluted flight through Montreal and Athens (Air Canada) then to Izmir (Aegean Air) might be the cause of the hiccup. But as it turns out we check in at the airport without a hitch and book our one suitcase all the way through to Izmir. And no extra fee for the suitcase either—thank you Lord!

Arriving at our gate nice and early we find just one person sitting there. Seems this woman speaks little or no English and is wondering where her plane is. She is at the gate marked on her boarding pass, but has not caught the announcements of a gate change. Betty is able to run with her to the new location just in time to see her on her flight. We know well enough what it is like to navigate a world we barely comprehend. We're on our way there right now. Betty is just "paying it forward."

In Montreal we are glad to discover our arrival gate is only 100 feet from our departure gate. So that is a handy connection, and we have only a short wait before boarding. But the flight to Athens is long and dreary, over nine hours. At least we have a good meal (again, without extra charge). But after the meal the lights go out, and with no individual control over reading lamps we can't read, or do sudokus. Neither can we pass the time with a movie since there are no screens. So we doze a little, talk a little, pray a little, until dawn breaks over Europe and we arrive at long last in sunny Athens.

As we step off the ramp into the airport we are greeted by the sign *Εξοδος* (*exodos* – exit). Ah, we are in Bible language territory. But this Greek has a few new words added that the apostle Paul and his kin would not have recognized, like τηλεφων (telephone). We peer through the glass at the hills and low mountains surrounding the airport. But no sign of the Areopagus, nor, alas, of the apostle preaching to the pagans. He could only serve his own generation, then pass the baton to others. May we be faithful in our own time, before we too pass on the Gospel baton.

Surprisingly we discover we get one hour of free wifi at the airport in Athens. Is this a legacy of the overly generous governments here that landed the country in economic hot water not too long ago? But I hear the country is turning around in that department. Anyway we gratefully log on to check email and find ourselves responding to a dear friend in Nova Scotia. Only now we discover that her husband had passed away in August. I worked for him almost 40 years ago as summer help on their dairy farm over-looking the Northumberland Strait and we have kept in touch ever since. We could not have imagined back then that we would be catching up with their news by email from Athens all these years later (I hope it arrives in English not Greek).

This is the time too, to sort out our currency. We won't need those Canadian dollars for a while. I tried to buy Turkish liras at the airport in Vancouver, but the exchange rate was terrible, 1.6 liras for one Canadian dollar. Fortunately they didn't have any liras on hand so we weren't tempted. I checked again in Montreal, same day, same company, and purchased liras at 1.8 per dollar—go figure! We can easily get more once we arrive in Turkey, but it is nice to have some on hand. We're also hoping to resurrect our old Turkish cell phone. Cell phone usage is cheap in Turkey, much cheaper than in Canada, but we may have to get a new sim card.

Colossians 1:1

Paul,
an apostle
of Christ Jesus
by the will of God

....

O Lord, who am I
that you should
remember me?

You have so many
appointments in your
day-timer. This vast
universe, sun and moon,
stars and planets, all on
their tight schedule.
Who are we?
Who am I? . . . to call
myself a Christ-one?

But you have done this.
You have made me so.
Grace upon grace.

O Lord, open my eyes to
see more of your glory
so that the contrariness
of my fellow travelers
will not intimidate me
into silence.

By your grace let me
wear your name large.

I pray in the name of
the crucified, risen,
ascended, reigning Jesus

Amen.

All Gift . . . All Grace

Right up front Paul identifies himself as an *apostle* of Christ—a *sent one*, a *missionary*. For Paul *apostle* is both title and job description, each firmly anchored in his relationship to Christ.

But is Paul not ashamed to be so closely associated with a crucified messiah? The cross was the most shameful death the Roman authorities could devise. Would not the followers of a crucified messiah also be a shameful tribe?

And how about us? Are we ever ashamed of Christ? After all, in our western societies, Christians are the butt of jokes, and the name of Christ is a common curse-word. And in a Muslim environment will we have the boldness to bear openly the name of Jesus?

So how encouraging it is to see Paul proudly carry the flag for our Lord. Here is a man who has seen the glory beyond the cross. He has met the very much alive Christ who so dramatically and powerfully turned him right side up on that road to Damascus. For Paul, the heavenly glory of Christ utterly eclipses any passing shame we might experience at street level.

By the way, is Paul bragging when he identifies himself as an apostle of Jesus? Absolutely not. To make that clear he immediately adds, "by the will of God." What an honest confession! Here is the man who earlier watched over the coats of those who stoned Stephen to death. But! . . . "by the will of God," he became servant of Christ. No, Paul is not bragging. He knows better than anyone that his life in Christ is all gift, all grace.

And is it not so for us also? Did not the Good Shepherd seek us long before we sought him? Was it not his Spirit who opened our eyes to the Light? Our life in Christ is all gift, all grace.

2. Arrival

We fly from Athens to Izmir in a Bombardier, a nice Canadian touch in a far off land. The small plane, like a caffeinated Canada goose, paddles excitedly to get off the runway, engines roaring. Will we clear the fence? We do, and climb slowly skywards for a marvellous view of the Aegean sea. The islands look to be ringed with ice, but as we watch closely we see it is not ice but breakers washing onto the shores. Some of those islands have ancient monasteries we know, but from 26,000 feet we can't tell what the large hilltop buildings are.

At some point we cross an invisible border and glide down to Izmir airport. Home at last—if you can call home a place where you need a visitor's visa. For the first time we have booked our visas ahead of time, over the internet, a new system. It costs $60 for a 3 month Canadian visitor visa. But no need to line up now at the visa wicket before heading for passport control. With our pre-purchased visa waiting for us somewhere in the digital universe we breeze through in record time. And it doesn't hurt that Izmir airport is much smaller than Istanbul. It's a great way to enter the county.

We travel the 20kms into the town center by rail. The train line runs right by the airport—how convenient is that? Except that the ticket counter is unmanned. Everyone seems to be using pre-loaded electronic passes which are available from vending machines, but we have no success in getting the machines to accept our money. Then a kindly man offers to let us through the gate on his card. We try to reimburse him the cost of the trip, but he refuses to accept our four liras. Welcome to Turkish hospitality. We thank him for his kindness. (Only later does it come to me that I might have given him a Turkish New Testament as a gift. O Lord, wake me up!) We gradually realize this train does not take us directly to the main Basmane train station. We will have to transfer. But again people are quick to help us know where we jump off to make the connection.

The city of Izmir may be better known to some of us as Smyrna of New Testament fame. The church of Smyrna was one of the seven churches of Revelation. Jesus commended this congregation for their faithfulness under persecution, and encouraged them to stay the course. Because of its strategic location and sheltered harbour Smyrna was an important city in Greek and Roman times, and has remained so to this day. The city is now the third largest in the country with four million inhabitants and continues to be a major import-export gateway for the region. Curiously, Izmir also has a reputation as a left-leaning, free-thinking city in this socially conservative country. Perhaps there is something about the air of a west coast that causes this phenomenon (think of Vancouver on the west coast of Canada, and the U.S. city of San Francisco further down the same coast).

And so by mid afternoon we arrive at the (pedantically named!) Walk In Hotel, just a short hike from the station.

Through the magic of the internet we have booked a room here based on the handy location and good reviews. It seems like a good choice. The efficient desk clerk is waiting for us, with our info printed and ready. The room is clean and quiet. The bathroom is super small, but adequate with lots of hot water. We are tired after the long commute, but we resist taking a nap since we want to get our systems used to the new time zone. After a shower, and shave for me, we head out onto the sunny street.

We are aiming for the sea wall, knowing from the map it is only 15 minutes distant on foot. On the way we pass a green metal door set in a high wall, with a sign: "Saint Polycarp." Is it a church building?—but we can see nothing over the high wall. Perhaps it is a grave site. A quick check online later on and we discover we had, in fact, walked by the walled compound of the Church of St. Polycarp. The ancient building had been reconstructed in 1620.

Polycarp is one of the many heroes of the early days of the church. He lived between AD70 and 155. He was a disciple of the Apostle John and later became bishop of Smyna. Irenaeus, in his youth, knew Polycarp and heard him teach. He held firmly to the teaching of the apostles in a time when various heresies were threatening to blow the churches off course. He was also known a model of integrity in financial matters. What a great pastor he was.

But Rome eventually caught up with Polycarp. He was arrested and charged with being a Christian. The Roman official in overseeing his case felt sorry for the old man and urged him to simply voice the words, "Caesar is Lord," and offer some incense at Caesar's statue. That was all he had to do to walk free. But Polycarp responded with these now famous words, "Eighty-six years I have served Christ, and he never did me any wrong. How can I blaspheme my King who saved me?" He was burned at the stake at Kadifkale, a hill near the center of modern Izmir.

No doubt Polycarp was encouraged by a line from the earlier letter of Jesus to the church there: "Do not fear what you are about to suffer . . . Be faithful unto death and I will give you the crown of life" (Revelation 2:10). What a memorable example of faithfulness for us as we face growing opposition as followers of Jesus in our own day.

That hill in Izmir is now home to a ruined castle. It is worth the journey to the top for the great view of the city and its wonderful, well-sheltered harbour, home to sea craft of all kinds, including NATO submarines and other warships, alongside container ships, fishing boats and cruise liners. Years earlier Betty and I had enjoyed that view as part of a tour group. But no time for that on this trip. After our long journey we have barely energy left for our stroll. But we enjoy the beauty of the seaside park and the sun low over the water.

I try out my lapsed Turkish on one of the guys fishing off the seawall. "İyi akşamlar!" "Good evening!" (Evening begins in the late afternoon in Turkey.) I ask him if he is catching anything. He says he has only just begun but he expects good fishing. Fishermen are optimists in any language.

We ask someone else for directions to the city's covered market, said to rival the Grand Bazaar in Istanbul. "Just 200 meters further on," we are told. It's a line we often hear in Turkey, and have learned to take it with a grain or two of salt.

Sure enough, two hundred steps further and the covered market is nowhere in sight. After a couple more inquiries we decide to forget about the market. But we do find a nice place to have dinner. It is a little upscale (i.e. "pricier") but it has a pleasant view over the water and the food is good. In this way we celebrate our safe arrival in this remarkable land.

On the way back to the hotel we get our old Turkish cell phone up and running. The new sim card and 200 minutes of talk time—more than enough to cover our trip—costs 35 liras ($20). We can call or text anywhere in Turkey for the same rate. Then we pause to look at some clothing spilling out onto the sidewalk. I can't resist a pair of dress pants for 20 liras. I need these for our trip anyway. For three more liras they are clipped and hemmed by a short and friendly tailor named Memet. Poor Betty is falling asleep as she sits on a stool and waits. I keep my eyes open talking to the young salesman who is from Trabzon, the "Newfoundland" of Turkey—strong of accent and brunt of many jokes. Then it is time to call it an early night.

Colossians 1:2a

To the saints and faithful brothers [and sisters] in Christ at Colossae

....

Heavenly Father, how good you are to us.

You have given us a place to call home in your vast universe, an address in Colossae, or Toronto, or Vancouver or. . . How blessed we are.

But more—you have given us a second address a home in Christ. "In the heart of Jesus, there's a place for you." How is this possible?

No loan application, no credit check or means test empty-handed, just as I am, without one plea you have prepared a place for me. What grace.

Forgive me Lord for hiding my unmeritability. For it is in my weakness that Christ is displayed, hope dawns for others.

Lord, help the homeless, even through me.

Amen

Saints Unmerited

We see that Paul is not simply writing to the *Christians* at Colossae, he is writing to the *saints* at Colossae! "What about the rest of the church?" we are tempted to ask. After all, have we ever met a church where every member is a saint? Has Paul never been to a church business meeting?! Besides, I know I am not a saint. Am I excluded here?

But then we recall that, for us now, the word saint has shifted in meaning since Paul's day. We have a long history of selecting above average Christians and labeling them alone as *saints* (like Saint Polycarp). This has become so ingrained in our religious language that we cringe at the thought of applying the term *saint* to ourselves.

So what should we do with this word saint? Are we to dial it down, so it fits the humblest of believers? Has the church over the past 2000 years raised the sainthood bar too high? Yet surely the very opposite is true, the bar has been set too low!

Paul's word *saint* means *special, spotless, consecrated, set apart for God's exclusive use.* It means, in fact, nothing less than *holy,* as God is *holy.* Paul is writing to the *holy ones* at Colossae, those who echo the very character of the Lord, crystal clean, utterly untainted by any sin!

How is that possible? Surely no normal human being merits that kind of sainthood.

But that is exactly the point. Our sainthood is precisely *un*-merited. It is a gift. It is grace. It is God who has made us saints. And he has done this through Christ. We are saints because we, like the church in Colossae, are hidden *in Christ* (1:2, 3:3).

How can Paul, that old rebel, be called an apostle? Yet he is, by the grace of God. How can we in our weakness, often failing, falling, be called saints? Yet we are. Saints by grace, Hallelujah!

3. On the Train

One of the great treats of staying in Turkish hotels is the breakfast that is usually included in the price of the room. The morning buffet at Walk In Hotel opens at seven and we are there soon after. Sitting down to fresh bread, boiled eggs, cucumbers, tomatoes, a variety of soft cheeses, olives, jams, honey, and the ever-present Turkish tea, we eat enough to do us until dinner (with just a wee small snack at noon.)

Other travelers are also eating breakfast. Some are Turks glued to the morning news on the overhead TV. Some have come from further afield—a Chinese family, and a few other westerners like ourselves. One woman has her nose bandaged. Some Turkish women feel they will look more attractive if they have cosmetic surgery to reduce the size of their ethnically generous nose. Possibly this woman has come to Izmir for such reasons. Is she longing for more acceptance, or seeking a boost to her self-confidence? I wonder if she will ever hear how precious she already is to her Heavenly Father, or if she will ever read these words in 1 Peter 3:3-4.

> *Do not let your adorning be external—the braiding of hair and the putting on of gold jewellery, or the clothing you wear—but let your adorning be the hidden person of the heart with the imperishable beauty of a gentle and quiet spirit, which in God's sight is very precious.*

After breakfast we have a few errands to run before leaving on the train for Denizli. We find a money exchange office that gives us over two liras per Canadian dollar—now we're talking! Then we walk past the Antik Han, an old hotel, full of character, where I and two other travelers stayed on a previous trip. A couple of blocks further and we arrive at the historic Smyrna *Agora*, the marketplace of ancient times. We pay the very modest entry fee and have a quick look around.

Not much has changed since our last visit but work slowly continues on resurrecting some impressive old buildings not yet open to the public. More than just a commercial centre for this busy port city, this place was also the judicial, political, artistic, and educational hub of the city. After the disastrous earthquake of AD178 it was rebuilt, though not perfectly—the arches don't quite line up. Nevertheless it is an impressive example of a multi-story shopping mall and city centrepiece preserved from early times.

So it's good bye to Izmir, a soft westernized portal into this culturally distant middle-eastern world. We leave a multi-lingual Christian DVD and a tip under the pillow for the housekeeper and tuck a Turkish *Life of St. Francis* into the drawer by the bed. Books have a good shelf-life. We pray this one will catch someone's eye when the time is right. Then we tow our belongings round the corner to the station.

Our combined train tickets to Denizli cost 36 liras. Because of my advanced age I am only responsible for the smaller half of that. Since the journey will take about four hours we pick up a bottle of water and a couple of *simit* (a sesame-seed-coated bread ring, the ubiquitous and delicious

Turkish street snack.) Betty finds a shady seat on the platform. I have time for a couple more photos of the historic Basmane railway building before departure.

Once the train pulls in we expect a mad rush for the doors, so we plan ahead as to where we will aim to sit. I guess that if we park on the left we will spend less time in the sun. Also we want to stay close to the luggage rack so we can keep an eye on our belongings. Turns out we needn't have worried about the rush. This train starts its journey only a quarter full. Betty easily claims prime seats. I stow the suitcase and we make ourselves comfortable as the train slowly pulls out of the station.

Leaving the city the train passes under the shadow of a massive, mountain-side sculpture of the face of Atatürk, the great post-WWI liberator, and father of modern Turkey. Curiously, this quintessential Turk was born in Thessalonica, outside the boundaries of present-day Turkey (though it was part of the aging Ottoman empire in those days). Across the countryside statues of Mustafa Kemal Atatürk are everywhere, but this, at 40 metres high, tops them all for size.

In fact the shadow of the great champion is still very much apparent across this the land. It was he who brought in the use of Roman script for written Turkish in 1928—we foreigners bless him for that change. Before that, Turkish (Ottoman Turkish) was written in a kind of Arabic script. Turkish itself is unrelated to Arabic, belonging to a very different linguistic family, but in olden times, as the once oral-only language looked for a written form, it was the Arabic script that lay close to hand. Atatürk also banned the fez, encouraged western dress and western music, and made Sunday the day of rest in a predominantly Muslim land. What a paradoxical place this is!

Our train stops at every station giving us lots of time to enjoy the sights. Through the windows we watch sad partings and joyous welcomes. We love these well-kept stations, nicely painted, often brightened with well-tended flowerbeds, and always the shaded *çay baçesi* (tea garden) close by. Trains arrived here a century and a half ago, and they are still very much a part of everyday life. In recent years high-speed lines are connecting more and more centres, we hope to try them out before we leave, but we do like the slow trains that give a leisurely view of the countryside.

On the first leg of our journey we travel almost south, to Selçuk, the modern stop-off town for old Ephesus. Amazingly much of this area would have been below sea level in the days when the Apostle Paul arrived in Ephesus by boat. Now the sea is eight kilometres away from the site of the old city. When we arrive at the familiar station of Selçuk we are tempted to jump off the train for one more look around the archaeological marvel which is Ephesus today. But our hotel in Denizli is booked and we have miles to go before we sleep.

From the window we enjoy the beautiful countryside of this Mediterranean coastal region. We follow first the Cayster river, then up over a minor pass to join the Meander river valley, traveling now eastward and inland. Yes, our modern word "meander" comes from the old Greek name of that wandering river. What a fertile landscape. Mile after mile of olives, grapes, other fruit of various kinds, all flourishing with water from the rivers and heat from the Mediterranean sun.

Many houses have walled gardens with pomegranates, figs, lemons, nut trees, and others we cannot name. We often see grape vines trained over backyard or roof-top trellises to provide shade from the burning summer heat. Sometimes the vines go straight up three or four stories, before being allowed to break out into a riotous green canopy. Occasionally we see a few dairy cows, and a couple of times sheep led by a shepherd, but this is not the place for much livestock farming.

From the train we see life differently than from the road. Trains run through the world's back yard. Is it the voyeur in us that enjoys the view from the train window? We glimpse into back yards, and warehouses. We see people in vulnerable emotional moments, like the child bouncing up and down in joy at the sight of his cousins getting off the train for a visit to their rural home. Later we realize that a couple days from now will be the Korban Bayramı, the Muslim Sacrifice Holiday, the biggest holiday of the year. The whole country seems to be traveling somewhere, family is so important.

As we near the end of our journey, a little tired and hungry despite our minor lunch preparations, an optimistic gentleman jumps on board selling *simit*, water, tea, and other refreshments. We purchase a couple of containers of *ayran*, a watery yogurt drink we find very refreshing in hot weather. After a healthy run of sales our friendly entrepreneur moves to the next car.

We know we are getting close when suddenly there are the famous white cliffs of Pamukale off in the distance. These are the massive calcium deposits of the famous hot springs of the area. The Turkish name Pamukale translates into "Cotton

Castle" and it's not hard to make that connection. Alongside Pamukale is the site of ancient Hierapolis, mentioned only in Colossians in the New Testament. And across the valley from Pamukale is the site of Laodicea, mentioned in Colossians and Revelation.

> *Epaphras, who is one of you, a servant of Christ Jesus, greets you, always struggling on your behalf in his prayers, that you may stand mature and fully assured in all the will of God. For I bear him witness that he has worked hard for you and for those in Laodicea and in Hierapolis (Colossians 4:12-13).*

It looks as though Epaphras, by God's grace, founded the church in nearby Colossae, and possibly also the churches in Laodicea and Hierapolis. He certainly loves them as a founder (or a mother) might, and continues to battle in prayer for them even when he is away. As the tracks swing right, out of the valley towards Denizli, we catch a glimpse of ruins of Laodicea on our left. At last we arrive at our destination. The train is such a great way to travel.

Colossians 1:2b

Grace to you and peace from God our Father
....

O Lord, forgive me for seeking peace apart from grace.

In my pride I resist saying yes to your grace. I cling to my independence, as a child clings to a candy wrapper.

Lift my head, O Lord. Pry my hands loose. Lead me to the well one more time.

For when I do let go and drink, how deeply your peace fills my heart.

And Lord, dare I ask, that I be a means of grace to other restless souls who, like me, persist in their paint-by-numbers religious quest, but find no haven?

O Lord, bring peace to this land... but first grace, first grace.

Grace to them, and peace.

Amen.

Through Grace, To Shalom

When Paul baptizes the traditional Greek letter-opening—"A to B, greetings"—he turns *chairein* ("greetings") into *charis* ("grace"). What an inspired moment! All of the Gospel can be summed up in that astonishing word "grace."

But even that is not enough for Paul. He just has to squeeze into his formula the lovely old Hebrew greeting, *shalom*, "peace" (in Greek it is *eirene*). And so Paul's unique "grace and peace" blessing becomes this unforgettable motif that sings though his letters.

Shalom is much more than the absence of conflict. *Shalom* is about health, wholeness, completeness, and a sense of well-being. Psalm 23 describes the Shepherd of our souls providing *shalom* for the flock—food and drink, rest and restoration. *Shalom* is not necessarily about the removal of trouble, but the Shepherd is comfortingly near in the darkest of days. He feasts us even in the presence of our adversaries. *Shalom* is also about looking forward to a blessed future, dwelling in His house, forever.

This is the gift of peace that comes to us now in Christ, this *shalom*, this experience of well-being, even during the darkest of times. Plus a future in his presence that we anticipate with hope and joy. This is the peace that passes understanding.

But notice the word order in Paul's blessing. Grace comes first. In fact the precise wording is always, "grace to you, and peace...." The priority of grace is underlined. Peace is almost an afterthought.

Is it possible to have peace without grace? Not the kind of peace we find in Christ. First we humble ourselves and come to him with empty hands and drink deeply from the heavenly reservoirs of grace. Then what peace, what *shalom*!

4. At Home in Denizli

With our trusty Google map to guide us we make our way out of the station and up a steep grade to street level. In front of us is one of the main arteries of the city and traffic is heavy. Crossing traffic is dodgy in Turkey, the law of tonnage prevails—the right of way ceded to the biggest. We wait for the light to change and cross with others, there is some safety in numbers, then head southwest towards the new bus terminal.

The city is proud of its new *oto gar* and rightly so. The intercity and regional buses load and unload their passengers on two below-ground levels. So instead of the usual unsightly and noisy loading area, all that is seen from above are smart offices and a green space with beautiful flower beds and seating areas.

Suddenly Betty spies our new home, the Business Address Hotel, just beyond the *oto gar*. Like our stop-over in Izmir it doesn't have a very romantic name, but the location is great and it promises a good-sized room for a reasonable rate. This will be home base for the best part of a week.

Why are we coming to this modern city of Denizli? Well, we want to include as part of our trip, some time in a place where there are few, if any, known Christians. At the time we booked our tickets we were not aware of any churches in this city of over half a million souls. Since then, however, we have discovered there is one small house church. We hope to visit them on Sunday. So we have simply come, in the name of Jesus, to enlarge the Christian presence in Denizli for a few days at least. We will pray and walk the streets. We will look for opportunities to talk. Perhaps, in some small way, we can participate in what God is already doing here. While here we do want to have another look at the two nearby ancient sites of Laodicea and Colossae, and remember a time when the Gospel was leaping from city to city all through these valleys. But mostly we want to be servants of our own generation.

The people who live here now are Turks. These people migrated into this region a thousand years after Epaphras brought the Gospel to Colossae. Only now, probably for the first time in their history, are these Turks at last hearing the Christian message. And slowly, across this land, brand new congregations of Turkish Christians are emerging. How God loves these people. He has held off on drawing the final curtain on planet earth wanting to gather this family also to their seats around the heavenly banquet table.

The Lord is not slow to fulfill his promise as some count slowness, but is patient toward you, not wishing that any should perish, but that all should reach repentance (2 Peter 3:9).

Unfortunately we don't get off to a very good start at the front desk at our digs in Denizli. The gentleman doesn't seem to know anything about our reservation. But he does have a room so we agree on a price and hand over our passports, as the law requires in this country. By the end of the day the police want to know the ID of every hotel guest in the land. Being young and hi-tech he doesn't seek out a photocopier, he simply photographs our passports with his "hand-held digital device" and passes them directly back to us. We get a key and navigate the tiny elevator to the second floor (on the fourth floor really, since the lobby and restaurant floors are not counted). The room is smaller than expected and certainly not very clean, but we decide it will do for now.

After a brief look around the neighbourhood to get ourselves oriented and pick up a few supplies, we enjoy a makeshift dinner in our room. It's time to check the news online and type up a few notes. Betty washes some clothes in the sink and we drape them over the furniture to dry overnight. (I need to buy a piece of rope to use as a clothesline.) Thank you Lord for our safe journey and a good beginning in this remarkable land.

Despite our strange surroundings we sleep well. Soon it is time to be heading off for another good breakfast. And then, the next order of business—to see about the room situation. I go down to the front desk with a printout of our reservation. We had purposely booked a corner room because, according to the website at least, the corner rooms are much more spacious than the tighter quarters we had been given. It's the same chap behind the desk, but he is trying to be helpful. Yes, there is a corner room, it will be ready in one hour. It turns out to be much more suitable and somewhat cleaner. I had been thinking about looking for another hotel, but with this change of rooms we decide to remain here for the rest of the week. It will do for our temporary home.

Colossians 1:3-6

We always thank God, the Father of our Lord Jesus Christ, when we pray for you
....

Dear Heavenly Father, Father of our Lord Jesus, we worship you, we thank you.

Thank you for bringing the Gospel to us, in our far-off land of Canada. Thank you for the beautiful feet of the Gospel bearers. Thank you for awakening my own heart when your Word came to me.

And thank you for these brothers and sisters in Turkey, for calling them to yourself, for this holy seed in a parched land.

You love these people more than we can imagine —a people to die for!

O Father of the One with the nail-scarred hands, thank you for the saints in this and that city.

Amen.

Thank You Lord

"We always thank God . . ." Paul continues. How fitting and appropriate. Can there be any healthier response to the outpouring of God's grace in our lives? Is there any better way to begin our prayers? When we pray "Thank you, Lord," we express our acceptance of his grace. It is a way of receiving and owning this unmerited gift. Thank you, Lord.

And we can pray this way for others also, as Paul is doing here. How encouraging this must have been for the small outpost of brothers and sisters in Colossae, living out their faith as a tiny minority in the shadow of a powerful, proud, pagan, Roman city. It must have been intimidating at times. Yet here is Paul giving thanks for them. Why?

Because God has chosen them, he has graced them, sanctified them. God has hidden them "in Christ." How precious they are to their Heavenly Father. Paul's thankfulness for them echoes the delight and joy of God over them.

And what is it like for the handful of Christians who live in Denizli today, the modern city of half-a-million people close to the site of old Colossae? Here in Canada we would close down a little group like that. But how precious they are in God's eyes. "We always thank God . . . when we pray for you."

What a faithful pray-er Paul is. Not *if* we pray for you, but *when* we pray for you. And not just a one-time prayer, but continuous, *always*, he writes.

We note also this is also such a well-directed prayer. Which god is Paul praying to? He is praying to the Father of our Lord Jesus Christ. He is praying not to a tree or a mountain, nor to a great idea, nor karma. Paul is praying to the one, true, living God, gloriously revealed in the face and life of Jesus.

How do we know God is so good? so praiseworthy? We look at Jesus, and we know.

5. A Visit to Old Colossae

Our chief assignment for this morning is to visit the site of ancient Colossae about 20kms out of town. There is a well-staffed tourist centre in the new *oto gar* but no one at the front desk seems to know anything about Colossae. Then a senior figure emerges from a back room and silently leads us out through the maze of regional mini-buses and points to one heading for Honaz. From my reading I know that after Colossae was abandoned, Honaz, earlier called Chonae, in the shadow of mount Cadmus, became the new population centre. We seem to be on the right track. This bus should pass the entrance to the old site of Colossae. We squeeze onboard and await departure. But how will we know where to get off the bus? Fortunately a friendly young lady in the seat ahead of us hears us talking and offers to tell us when to disembark.

And that is how we come to find ourselves in the middle of nowhere, on the side of a dusty country road, our bus disappearing into the distance, looking at a faded sign announcing "Kolosse." Beyond the sign a rough path ascends a small hill. There is no gate or ticket office, in fact we appear to be completely alone as we wander over the mound of the old city site. It is hard to believe now but this was once a large and flourishing city on a major highway. By the time of Christ, however, it was already playing second fiddle to Laodicea and Hierapolis. The Romans had built a new road and Colossae got by-passed—an old and familiar story.

So far there has been almost no archeological work done in Colossae, which means there is not a lot to see. Perhaps this will change soon as Turkey wakes up to the possibilities of "faith tourism." Tomorrow we want to see where the Laodicea dig is up to after all the recent work on that site. But here in Colossae we can only imagine what the city must have been like. Nevertheless it is thrilling to think that in this place, 2000 years ago, there were followers of Jesus. And we have a letter written to them by the Apostle Paul, plus his more personal letter written to Philemon, also of Colossae. Where was the home where the church met, that Paul mentions in that letter? What did Philemon do for a living?

And how did Epaphras become a Christian? We suppose it was while Paul was teaching in Ephesus during his extended ministry there. Very likely Epaphras had gone into the big city on business and there heard the Gospel from the great apostle. Back in Colossae he couldn't help but share with his family and friends the wonderful story of Jesus. And so a new congregation was born. This is how the Good News spreads.

> *And he [Paul] entered the synagogue [in Ephesus] and for three months spoke boldly, reasoning and persuading them about the kingdom of God. But when some became stubborn and continued in unbelief, speaking evil of the Way before the congregation, he withdrew from them and took the disciples with him, reasoning daily in the hall of Tyrannus. This continued for two years, so that all the residents of Asia heard the word of the Lord, both Jews and Greeks (Acts 19:8-10).*

In our explorations we come across the old amphitheatre. Very few of the stone seats remain in place, but the semi-circle is plain to see. We try to imagine Philemon and his friends Apphia and Archippus (possibly wife and son?) taking in a Greek play on a Friday evening, out under the stars. Perhaps with Onesimus the slave hovering in the background to bring refreshments to his master as required. After Paul sent Onesimus back home, no longer just a slave, but also a brother in Christ, possibly he got to sit alongside his master. It must have been a bit awkward at times—is he a slave, or is he a brother? We wonder if, after their conversion, they decide the Greek plays are inappropriate. At least they will have to be more discerning about what they allow their eyes and ears to take in as they keep their hearts pure for Christ.

Then, suddenly, as we are wandering around old Colossae, three Gendarmes show up, smartly dressed, but well armed. Someone has phoned to say strangers are walking around up there. Odd though, since this is an open, well-marked historic site. Anyway they are very friendly. We have a little chat in my meagre Turkish. Then they ask if we are husband and wife. When I say yes they seem satisfied and take off! We remember that earlier, from the hilltop, we had looked down on a farmer working his orchard. Betty noticed that when he saw us he turned around and made a call on his cell phone. Did he think we were having a furtive rendezvous? Or was he just tired of having foreigners stare down on his work? I guess I was holding Betty's hand as we climbed up and down over the rocks. But then, we have been married a long time, and have the grandchildren photos to prove it.

Eventually, camera loaded with shots of every rock and vista, we climb down the steep track that leads off the site. To get back to Denizli we must wait at the side of the lonely road for the next mini-bus. Ah, here it comes. We wave and the driver stops for us and we head back to the *oto gar* and our nearby hotel. And that's how you visit Colossae. For the record you catch the bus for Honaz at platform #15 at the amazing new multi-story bus terminal. Buses leave every 15 minutes and the ride costs four liras per person, one way.

Back at the hotel we take a little siesta. Then we set out, mid-afternoon, to find the old market area called Kaleiçi (lit. "inside the castle"). We see no sign of an old castle, but we do eventually find the rabbit warren of covered little streets lined with small-time vendors. We buy some rope for a clothesline for our laundry. But we are mostly looking for a new suitcase. The wheels are falling off the one we brought with us. Unfortunately we see everything but suitcases—clothing of all kinds, footwear, bulk tea, electronics, hardware, a short street of tinsmiths their fires blazing—but no suitcases.

On the way back we pass a little restaurant called Çobanoğlu, "son of the shepherd," what a nice name. Back in the hotel, after a little online searching, I realize we are not far from a modern shopping mall. After a some homemade supper in the hotel room we hike our way over there. At last we find suitcases, but why so expensive? We decide to wait with that purchase. We don't stay long. The shopping mall is the same as a million shopping malls the world over. The old market area is much more interesting. We'll go back later for another look.

Colossians 1:7-8

you learned it from Epaphras our beloved fellow servant. He is a faithful minister of Christ on [our] behalf and has made known to us your love in the Spirit.

....

Forgive us Father when we grumble about the new carpet, and fuss over the new music, and gossip about the un-tie-d pastor or "irreverent" children.

Is Christ exalted?
—Hallelujah!
Is the Word honoured?
—Hallelujah!
Is His Gospel preached?
—Hallelujah!

O Father may I leave in my wake not a trail of destruction but a trail of construction of warm encouragement.

How quickly I will pass from this earth. Let me serve the next generation as well as this.

Bless you, Epaphras!

Amen

A Ministry of Encouragement

There is a lovely warmth to this letter. But we wonder where that tenderness comes from. This is not one of Paul's daughter churches. He had only a second-hand knowledge of them (1:4, 9), he had not met them personally (2:1). Then it comes to us . . . this is Paul's granddaughter church, perhaps the very first. And those of us who are grandparents know how cherished grandchildren are!

During his extended stay in Ephesus Paul seems to have tried a new church planting strategy. Perhaps he was already sensing he didn't have much time left. What would happen to the mission after he was gone? So in Ephesus he focused on training others who would go out and train others (see 2 Timothy 2:2).

And his strategy was a resounding success. New congregations sprouted up all over Asia Minor. And the church in Colossae is a marvelous case study. Praise God, the mission of bringing the Gospel to the world would not die with Paul! He saw already the baton being passed on to the next generation. No wonder he writes to Colossae with such delight.

So we see the tenderness of Paul towards the sisters and brothers there. But we also see the warm words he has for Epaphras who had brought the Gospel to them. This man is a "beloved fellow servant . . . a faithful minister of Christ." And later Paul speaks of Epaphras as a tireless prayer warrior, who has laboured so hard for the churches in Colossae, Laodicea, and Hierapolis (4:12, 13).

Are we known as those who encourage the next generation? True, their ministry may not look like our ministry. And they don't do things exactly the way we did. But if they are faithful servants of Christ seeking only his will for the church (4:12) let's cheer them on. Even Paul could do that!

6. And a Visit to Laodicea

Breakfast in the hotel here is standard Turkish fare, not quite the generous spread we have seen elsewhere, but not bad. We have been starting the day with a hard-boiled egg, lots of bread and cheese, jam and halva, and plenty of Turkish tea to wash it all down. Friday morning we sleep in somehow, perhaps part of our adjustment to local time, and come down to find the buffet all cleaned away. But a few plates remain with food already picked out for us. Not quite the selection we would have made, but adequate. Tomorrow we will be up earlier!

It seems the hotel has few clients at the moment. No foreigners here, and very few couples. Mostly single guys traveling on business we assume. It's not a very friendly place. It is hard even to make eye contact, everyone keeps to themselves, eats quickly, then moves on. We try to follow the news on the TV. At least we get the weather, which is a sunny 25°C day after day—not bad for October.

Today we want to go to Laodicea. We skip the shiny new tourism office next door to the bus terminal, they haven't been too knowledgeable anyway, and go straight to the bus information table in the heart of the cavernous traveler's lounge. We are promptly directed to platform #76 where a mini-bus is waiting for the run to Pamukale.

These local buses are quite new-looking, clean and bright, with seating for about 20 passengers. Many are made by Mercedes. It is comforting to ride in buses that look reasonably new and appear well-maintained. We take our seats and wait for the *kapitan*, the driver. When he comes I ask him to give us the nod when we get to the drop off for Laodicea. This is necessary since, once again, we don't really know where we are going. Only two liras each for this trip. Along the way the *kapitan* stops to take more passengers on board until we become sardine-like in our sociable coziness.

As it turns out I spot the sign for Laodicea coming up just as the driver catches my eye in the mirror. And suddenly here we are, once again alone under the hot sun, setting off up a little side-road that presumably takes us to our destination. But it is an enjoyable walk with a village feel, small farms on either side, a few orchards, a cheerful stream nearby. A friendly-looking older woman is sorting out her laundry in her back yard. "*Kolay gelsin*," we call out. This is a polite idiomatic expression meaning something like, "May it [your work] come easy." She is obviously pleased with her two foreigners. "*Hoş geldiniz!*" she calls back ("Welcome [to our place]!") We call back the obligatory response. This is the friendly face of Turkey we have come to know and love.

As we continue we pass close to a pomegranate tree loaded with fruit. We take only pictures. Then, as we pause to enjoy the scene, a passing car slows down. We think the kindly driver wants to offer us a lift. But we wave him on. The entrance to the historic site of Laodicea is just ahead. Walking up to the wicket we surprise the occupant. He had heard no tour bus, nor even a car. I suppose not too many people just walk in.

But he accepts our 10 liras each with a smile and we continue our hike up into the heart of the site.

Old Laodicea has changed dramatically since Betty and I were first here ten years ago as part of a tour group. We recall there was no admission fee then, not even a guard to monitor the place. It was basically a hilltop with a few old square stones poking through what was otherwise a sheep pasture. There had been a few modest archaeological surveys carried out over the years, including one (1961-63) by Dr. J. des Garniers of Quebec university. But there was little to suggest the grandeur of Laodicea in its heyday. On that visit we had explored the two ruined amphitheatres and looked across the valley to Pamukale with its hot springs, and nearby Hierapolis. But there wasn't much else to see.

Well, what a difference a decade makes! Under the direction of Dr. Celal Şimşek of Pamukale university the archaeological work has forged ahead. The main entrance street has been uncovered. Enough of the agora has been exposed to for us to see the immense size of it, a reminder that Laodicea was a major trade hub. Just in the last year a set of massive, well-preserved columns has been unearthed. We were able to get a glimpse into the deep pit where these are still being examined by workers. Nearby, enough of a great temple has been re-erected for us to get a sense of the size and beauty of the edifice.

Even more exciting was the discovery in 2011, by the use of ground-penetrating radar, of a well-preserved church building. According to the chief archaeologist this building dates from the reign of Constantine (306-337). It has 11 apses, one facing east, the remainder north and south. The floor has both floral and geometric mosaics. And the cross-shaped marble (full-emersion) baptistery is considered to be one of the best preserved from this early period.

Unfortunately we are not able to walk through the remains of the church itself as it is still under reconstruction. But we can get a sense of the size and complexity of the structure. The local powers that be are waking up to the tourism potential of a more developed Laodicea site. The newly discovered church building is being billed as, "the Sacred Cross Church, one of the seven churches mentioned in the Holy Bible." More accurately, of course, this building would have been erected by the descendents of that church.

We remember the famous words of Jesus to that church, penned by the apostle John in Revelation chapter three:

> [14] *"And to the angel of the church in Laodicea write: 'The words of the Amen, the faithful and true witness, the beginning of God's creation.*
>
> [15] *"'I know your works: you are neither cold nor hot. Would that you were either cold or hot!* [16] *So, because you are lukewarm, and neither hot nor cold, I will spit you out of my mouth.* [17] *For you say, I am rich, I have prospered, and I need nothing, not realizing that you are wretched, pitiable, poor, blind, and naked.* [18] *I counsel you to buy from me gold refined by fire, so that you may be rich, and white garments so that you may clothe yourself and the shame of your nakedness may not be seen, and salve to anoint your eyes, so that you may see.* [19] *Those whom I love, I reprove and discipline, so be zealous and repent.* [20] *Behold, I stand at the door and knock. If anyone hears my voice and opens the door, I will come in to him and eat with him, and he with me.* [21] *The one who*

conquers, I will grant him to sit with me on my throne, as I also conquered and sat down with my Father on his throne. ²² *He who has an ear, let him hear what the Spirit says to the churches.'"*

The name, Laodicea, goes back to the 3ʳᵈ century BC when Antiochus II named the city in honour of his wife, Laodice. The city was devastated by the great earthquake of AD60 but in their wealth and pride they refused the financial rebuild funds offered by Rome. They could rebuild their own city, thank you. And they did, bigger and better than ever. The second theatre was built at that time. Strabo, the Greek historian of the first century mentions that Laodicea had a famous medical school. Some students of the New Testament wonder if Luke trained there. We note that Paul includes greetings from Luke in his letter to the church in Colossae at the point when he asks them to share his letter with the church in Laodicea. Could that be because they would have known him from his time there? (see Col. 4:14-16).

Even though we are only looking at the time-worn wreckage of that old city it is not hard to imagine the wealth alluded to in Jesus' evaluation letter. But *outer* wealth does not equal *inner* wealth. Spiritually they are impoverished. They might deal in the finest of woollen products but spiritually they are naked. They might produce the finest of eye salve, but spiritually they are as blind as a bat. They are about as desirable as a cup of tepid water, neither refreshing like the cold springs of Colossae up river, nor invigorating like hot springs of Hierapolis and Pamukale across the valley. They have become estranged from Jesus. And the only solution is to repent and turn back to him.

Is Jesus far away? No, he is near, he is close by, he has not abandoned them. But they have shut him out. Now is the time to open the door and invite him back into their lives, before it is too late, and the flame dies out completely.

So how did the church in Laodicea respond to Jesus' call. It seems they listened and obeyed. History records that Laodicea later became an important Christian religious center, being home to a bishop. In AD363-4 clergy gathered from across the region for the Council of Laodicea, which dealt with ethical and theological matters, including specifying the make-up of the biblical canon. Though curiously they did not include the book of Revelation in their collection at that time. With the recent discovery of the "Sacred Cross" church building we may now have the very place where the council was held.

All this is a reminder that God is not just in the business of beginning new churches, he is also in the business of bringing dead churches back to life. After all, is he not in the resurrection business?

As for the city itself it continued for another thousand years. But it was weakened by earthquakes and power struggles until the site was eventually abandoned.

By two o'clock Betty and I have had enough of wandering over dead rocks under the hot sun. We visit the gift shop and the clean, new toilets. Then head back down the hill, past the gatehouse, and back along that little country road—Laodicea is certainly not on the main highway today. When we get as far as the friendly lady in her back yard, Betty notices a faded sign announcing *Lokantı*, Restaurant. We make our way in beneath the pomegranate trees and through the garden gate. There are tables set up under the trees, and what looks like an open kitchen. But it turns out the people closed the restaurant some time ago and have neglected to take down the sign. We notice the woman's hands are decorated with henna, no doubt in celebration of something special coming up.

And so we make our way back out to the highway. After a short wait, sure enough a bus appears headed for Denizli. We wave and he stops, and we squeeze in and hold on for dear life in the crush. The *kapitan* will make money on this run. Tired and hungry, we limp back to the hotel, stopping for *Iskender Döner*, a famous hot meat dish on the way, complete with *ayran* and some *şalgam* for me (a sour drink originating from Adana, our next port of call).

Colossians 1:9-12

bearing fruit in every good work and increasing in the knowledge of God

....

Heavenly Gardener (may I call you that?) thank you for tending the plot of my own heart.

What a mess I got myself into, and still not all sorted, that's for sure.

But you have been at work in me, pruning (painful pruning), weeding out what has no place there, training my life in new directions.

What is that? An apple? An apple! Look! Look!

O Lord, I want to bear fruit for you. You can do this thing. Don't give up now.

And teach me to care for the garden of your church.

I pray in the name of the One who was once mistaken for a gardener on that brightest of all mornings.

Amen.

Tending the Garden

Those of us who love gardening love Genesis chapter two. "The Lord God planted a garden in Eden, in the east." And he took the man he had made, "and put him in the garden of Eden to work it and keep it" (Genesis 2:8, 15). What did he do? He planted, he watered, he weeded, he fertilized, he pruned, he fenced out the cattle, and he harvested.

Even before the sorry rebellion of the following chapter, the garden needed tending. Otherwise it would have been an unproductive mess. How much more so after the great Fall.

And churches need tending too. We are used to the metaphor of *shepherd* or *pastor* for a church leader. "Tend my sheep," Jesus instructed repentant Peter (John 21:16). But we have the metaphor of the *gardener* also. "I planted," Paul wrote, "Apollos watered, but God gave the growth" (1 Corinthians 3:6). Yes, God gives the increase, but he calls on his people to tend the crop.

How carefully Paul instructs Timothy in the care of the church in Ephesus (1 Timothy)—tending, feeding, leading, protecting, organizing. It is a joyful, but never-ending task.

What happens when the gardening is neglected? This is the story of the Laodicean church by the end of the first century. They had run wild, gone to seed, been overrun by invasive weeds. They had become a place of danger not shalom, a place of ugliness instead of beauty and holiness.

So here we see Paul's long-distance gardening of the Colossaean church—gardening by prayer. Yes, they have been planted well. Now he prays that that they will live *worthy of the Lord, pleasing to him, increasing in knowledge of God, bearing fruit, strengthened with all power,* and so experiencing *endurance, patience,* and *joy* (vs. 9-11).

7. On the Eve of Sacrifice

After a rest and an email check we head out again into the late afternoon to search once more for that elusive suitcase. Back to the covered market for a second time, for a more thorough search this go around. Finally we spy a luggage shop, we just hadn't gone far enough the first time. And the price is reasonable too. I bargain a little, but not too hard. The woman running the place needs the cash more than we do. She will be pleased to get one last sale before closing time. We head off down the street with our treasure, picking up some fruit along the way, pomegranates (which turn out to be barely ripe), and grapes (which are seedless and sweet). This, and some bread and cheese, will take care of our evening meal.

I am proud of my good wife. She seems content to wander with me around this distant part of the world. No doubt because she is well attuned to the ever-presence of the Lord. We've had no meaningful conversations with folks here yet. But we are present in the name of our *Christus Victor*. The church in Denizli has been enlarged, if only temporarily, during our stay! This is a great privilege for us. What will we leave behind?— some Christian reading material in Turkish and much prayer, and perhaps we can do more yet. For this short while, for all the unseen spirit-world to see, we are honouring Jesus in this place, and, we pray, some here below will see also.

Over the last couple of days we have noticed a number of knife sharpening enterprises set up street-side around town, extension cords snaking across the sidewalk, electric motors whirring, sparks flying. Also a number of impressive arrays of gleaming new knives in shop displays. At the same time we have seen sheep for sale here and there, and many trucks passing by with one or two or more sheep in the back. On our Friday evening walkabout we see a number of sheep tied up outside homes along the street. One man sits on his doorstep with his young son. They are talking together and looking over the sheep they have just bought. My guess is that he is explaining to his son the meaning of tomorrow's sacrifice. We exchange a greeting and a smile as we pass by.

For tomorrow is *Kurban Bayramı*, the Muslim sacrifice holiday. We had not anticipated this when we booked our tickets. But it does add another layer of intensity to our stay here. O Lord remember this people and their endless sacrifices. May they come to know you, Jesus, the Lamb of God, the One True Sacrifice, who takes away the sins of the world.

All across Turkey, sheep and goats, and cattle for the rich, will be slaughtered in memory of Abraham sacrificing the lamb in place of his son Ishmael (as they think). This year, as usual, vast numbers of animals will be sacrificed across the country. Every family will do their best to have their own lamb, or at least get together with a neighbour, if they are poor. These days the cities like to have the butchering done in central areas, but many animals are still killed in back yards and empty lots. The meat is then divided into three portions—one being given to the poor, one to neighbors and relatives, and the third being kept for the household. In recent years, some Muslims have begun to make donations to charitable institutions instead of personally sacrificing animals.

Kurban Bayramı is the main holiday of the year in Turkey spreading out over 4 or 5 days. The start date varies of course, back-tracking by about 10 days each year as it follows the lunar calendar like other Islamic religious days. So visitors might be surprised by this event in any season, depending on the year.

For working Turks, who rarely have a day off, this is a highly anticipated time, as much a celebration and family time as a religious holiday. It is a time for people to go back home, wherever home is. And all across Turkey, intercity buses, trains, and planes are booked solid. For those who don't travel this is still a time for friends and neighbours to visit each other. Hosts will offer cologne, candy and Turkish coffee. Children might be given pocket money. Those of the humbler class, like apartment building custodians, maids and gardeners may also receive a tip. There is a climate of generosity and warmth.

Another tradition is visiting the graves of deceased family members. This is mostly done one day prior to the *bayram*. The cemeteries are crowded with the living as well as the dead on that day.

How do people feel about all this shedding of blood? For most it is simply part of the only world they have ever known. In fact, for Betty and I, living so much of our life on the farm, and raising animals for food, it does not seem so strange either. We know how the steak gets to the meat counter at the supermarket. It is only the concept of endless, religious sacrifice that is foreign to us.

Interestingly we come across this news story a couple of days later:

A heart-warming story from Turkey has made headlines amid the sacrificial bloodshed, after 73-year-old Teyfik Gülay could not bring himself to slaughter the ram he purchased six months ago, instead deciding to keep it as a pet.

The soft-hearted old Gülay, who lives with his son in the north-western province of Bursa, bought another animal for the holy Feast of Sacrifice.

The ram he bought six months ago, which he has named "Murat," now lives in the small garden of his flat, after unexpectedly turning into a kind of pet while Gülay fed it for the six months leading up to the sacrifice. It began to accompany him everywhere he went, even joining him for breakfast.

When Murat began walking with him to the supermarket, Gülay finally understood he would not have the heart to have him killed. Gülay bought a bow tie for Murat, before taking him to visits to friends and relatives, a holiday tradition in Turkey but generally for humans only. Gülay told Doğan News Agency that he would feed Murat "until the end of his life."

Photos of the pensioner with Murat went viral over the first two days of the feast, receiving particular praise from animal lovers on Oct. 4, World Animal Day.

(from the Doğan News Agency, 5 October, 2014)

Curiously, one sheep laid down his life for another! Back here in Denizli we notice the shops closing up early on the eve of the holiday. We remember to stock up on a few additional food items knowing from experience that tomorrow almost everything will be closed. Then, tired but content, we head back to our room. We will sleep well tonight.

Colossians 1:13-14 — Ransomed, Healed, Restored, Forgiven

He has delivered us from the domain of darkness and transferred us to the kingdom of his beloved Son, in whom we have redemption, the forgiveness of sins.

The domain of darkness . . . the kingdom of his beloved Son—could there be any starker contrast?

Darkness is the domain of satan, a place of tyranny, of slavery, of oppression. But we must not give darkness too much credit. Darkness is not something in itself, it is merely the absence of light, the absence of truth and moral understanding. This is the world we live in apart from God.

But Christ has come to call us "out of darkness into his marvelous light" (1 Peter 2:9). Hallelujah! His kingdom is a place of light, and joy, and hope, and freedom. It is also a relational kingdom—the kingdom of *his beloved Son*. Here we dwell in a land of *belovedness* where we share in the love of the Father for his children.

How is this possible? Well, *Christus Victor* (to use the ancient Latin title), has crushed our enemy and rescued us from sin and death. It is another exodus moment—only greater. For not only did he rescue us, he also *transferred* us, air-lifted us, to his own kingdom. He didn't just extract us from darkness, he brought us home to himself.

But again, how is this possible? Verse 14 points to the deeper answer: in Christ we have *redemption*. We have been ransomed, a payment has been made, and we are forever free. This payment was totally out of our reach. But Christ has paid it for us. "In him we have redemption through his blood, the forgiveness of our trespasses, according to the riches of his grace" (Ephesians 1:7).

"Behold, the Lamb of God," said John the Baptist pointing to Jesus (John 1:29). Yes, the blood of the Lamb was poured out on the ground for our redemption. What a strange and glorious victory!

Praise, my soul, the King of heaven,
to the throne thy tribute bring . . .

Lord Jesus,
Lamb of God
who takes away
the sins of the world
I kneel before you with
praise and thanksgiving.

I recognize and confess
that I was complicit in
my own darkness
needing deliverance
not just from the evil one
but also from my own sin.

And now
you have ransomed me
by your own red blood.
Grace upon grace.

O Lord, may our new
neighbours track the blood
of these sheep and goats
to your own blood
spilled out once for all.

Amen.

8. A Divine Appointment

Sure enough, Saturday morning comes with unusual quiet. From the hotel window we see that instead of the normally unceasing rush and blare of car horns there is very little traffic on the streets. Though we are early for breakfast, just a few plates of food are set out. Not enough business this morning to warrant a buffet. But a friendly young man does come over to our table to say hello. He tells us he is a grape farmer, in town for the holiday. No wife yet, unfortunately.

But we are not going to stay inside like the rest of this city. We plan to walk over to a new, and apparently very beautiful park, "the most beautiful park in Turkey," according to the city brochure. How strangely quiet the streets are as we set out. For once the city is focused on family and friends, and on sober duties of Korban Bayramı. As we head out of the hotel we don't go far before we see carcasses hanging from a tree or a light pole. Some neighbours work on their projects together. In another place we see a sacrifice (dis)assembly line, the live animals solemnly looking ahead for a preview of their own demise. Children and cats watch from a distance. A number of times we sidestep blood on the sidewalk. After the sacrifice some carcasses are taken to the local butcher to be cut up professionally. Most will be dispatched on the kitchen table.

Red meat is very expensive here and none of this meat is wasted. It is shared around the neighbourhood with the very poor not forgotten. When we lived this country we were given some too, which we ate with thanksgiving and a free heart. In fact, for a few days, there is a glut of meat. We see an article in the newspaper warning people not to over-do their meat-eating, and not to over-dose on the sugary deserts that also go with this holiday time. When we watch the evening news we see the video clips of the ones that try to get away, the bulls running down main street or through back gardens, chased by embarrassed owners. It happens every year.

As we make our way across the city, following my roughly sketched map cribbed from Mr. Google, we meet a few others, couples and families, out for a holiday stroll. We follow custom and wish them *"İyi Baramlar,"* or *"Bayramınız kutlu olsun"*—variations on "Happy Holiday." People are pleased that we, obvious foreigners that we are, seem tuned in to their special day. One or two opportunistic shop-keepers have their doors open for anyone wanting a loaf of bread, or a bottle of perfume. But for the most part the shutters are down and the doors locked. I don't think we see more than one or two little eateries open. On the return journey we find a place that can sell us some ice cream, just what we need by noontime on a hot day. But that is all secondary to what the Lord had arranged for us on this day.

On the way to the park we come to an intersection with a huge glass sculpture of a rooster at the centre. The Denizli rooster is a distinct breed famous for its prolonged crowing and brilliant colours. It is the symbol of city and shows up everywhere. We take a couple of photos of this remarkable icon of the city, others are doing the same, then we move on. Walking down the street I notice that even the manhole covers have an outline of a rooster at the center of the circle. As I stop to snap a photo of a reasonably clean sample I notice two guys glancing our way. Soon after, as they come alongside us, one of the guys says to us, in English, "You look like foreigners." With a sheepish grin I confess, "Yes, I guess the folks who live here don't often take pictures of manhole covers!"

We chat a little more as we walk together. It turns out they are also going to the famous park. We soon discover they are Iranian refugees who have been in Turkey for a year.

"It must be very difficult for you here," I comment, knowing the severe restrictions placed on refugees in Turkey.

Then the talkative one (turns out the other speaks neither English nor Turkish) says, "It is difficult. But I love this place, because it is here that I met Jesus!"

Wow! What are the odds of meeting disciples of Jesus on the streets of this city?! And so our conversation takes off. We tell them we too are Christians and they are delighted to meet a couple of fellow believers. Together we walk into the park and find a place in the shade to sit and rest.

Always cautious in Turkey, because things may not be as they seem, we wait a while before eventually asking their names. The talkative brother turns out to be Peyman, his friend is Hamid. Peyman tells us, to our surprise and joy, that there are many Christian Iranians in Denizli. This had not occurred to us. We had heard there were very few Turkish believers here, but we had not anticipated the possibility that people of other backgrounds might name the name of Jesus in this city.

Later we remember the Lord's comforting words to Paul in his loneliness in Corinth:

> *And the Lord said to Paul one night in a vision, "Do not be afraid, but go on speaking and do not be silent, for I am with you, and no one will attack you to harm you, for I have many in this city who are my people." And he stayed a year and six months, teaching the word of God among them (Acts 18:9-11).*

These brothers speak openly of their longing to return to their homeland. Peyman misses his mother. But for now and the foreseeable future it is simply not safe for them to return. As they talk about their experiences in Iran and Turkey it is clear that through all their troubles, their hope and trust is in Jesus. Their joy is deeper than their sorrow.

Unfortunately we have not brought with us any Christian literature in Farsi, or in English. But I do have a multilingual DVD with two stories, one of Paul's conversion, the other of Mary Magdalene. They can watch it themselves then pass it on if they have an opportunity. I tell them God has sent them here to tell the Turks about Jesus. But I don't think they believe me. Besides, my Turkish seems better than theirs.

They are not aware of the little church in Denizli so I give them the contact info. Since this is all readily available on the internet I don't think I am giving away too many secrets. On a bridge over the pond in the park we take some photos. Then Peyman asks us to pray and we hold hands in a circle. Betty and I feel very conspicuous as we stand there out in the open for all to see. I pray first, then Peyman prays. How amazing is the love of God, that we find the family of God wherever we go! Somehow we say good bye and part.

As we walk away a friendly couple greets us from a park bench. I give them the Bayram greeting and they are pleased. How do you know it is the Bayram they ask. I tease them by saying the Denizli rooster seems to have slept in this morning and so the city also is still asleep. Turns out he is a doctor. He asks where we are from and what I do. But when I tell him that I am a pastor that seems to bring the conversation to a close. He is still smiling, but he is also clearly wanting us to move on. Perhaps he is afraid we will pray with them as he has just seen us pray with the other gentlemen just a short distance away. At least in some way we have identified ourselves as followers of Jesus.

And so we make our way back to the hotel, trying to figure out which streets we came on. Part way there we find a little store open and buy some ice cream, two Magnums to celebrate! There are a few more people out on the street now, but no one is rushing, it still feels very much like a holiday. Passing by the large glass rooster again we notice a Burger King, then a little later on a McDonalds. This must be the upper-class neighbourhood of Denizli, where anything western has *cachet*. The shops look expensive in this area too.

But then, up a little side street, we see an old man selling fruit off the back of a truck. Earlier we had bought some pomegranates that turned out to be dry and sour, despite the assurances of the vendor to the contrary. I ask this man if his pomegranates are juicy. He is honest enough to say no. I think he is saying that the season is still too early. But we do buy a very nice melon from him, dark green, but tasting like a honeydew melon.

Colossians 1:15-20

He is the image of the invisible God.
....

*Lord Jesus,
we kneel alongside our
"doubting" brother Tom
who first addressed you as
"My Lord and my God!"*

*It was no sheep
raised on the hills
sold from the bazaar
carried bleating home
slaughtered in the garden
watched over by the cats.*

*It was you
very God of very God
who bled out
for me
very sinner
of very sinner.*

*Amazing Love!
How can it be,
that thou, my God,
shouldst die for me?!*

*Lord Jesus,
may your divinity
shine through my words
and my behaviour.*

*For the sake of these
drinking their coffee
around me now.*

Amen.

Very God Of Very God

Some of us are so used to the reality that Jesus is divine we have difficulty remembering he is also human. He bruised when he hit his thumb with a hammer, he gained weight during the feast days in Jerusalem, he laughed at his own jokes.

But for those who first met Jesus, and for many later, the greater difficulty was to recognize his full divinity. Jesus stuns the religious leaders by forgiving a man of his sins. "Wait a minute," they protest, "that's God territory!" (Mark 2:5-7).

But Jesus, by his life and words, leaves us with no other conclusion. And in his letter to the church at Colossae Paul describes his Lord in soaring, divine superlatives—*the image of the invisible God . . . creator of all things . . . before all things . . . the head of the body, the church . . . the beginning . . . the firstborn from the dead . . . in everything preeminent . . . for in him all the fullness of God was pleased to dwell . . .* Glory!

How moving it is to visit Nicea (now called Iznik) in western Turkey. In this beautiful setting, on the shores of that quiet lake, the church fathers carefully and prayerfully worked on the precise wording of what would later become known as the Nicean Creed, which reads in part:

I believe . . .
. . . in one Lord Jesus Christ,
the only begotten Son of God,
begotten of his Father before all worlds,
God of God, Light of Light,
very God of very God,
begotten, not made,
being of one substance with the Father;
by whom all things were made;
who for us men and for our salvation
came down from heaven . . .

9. Another Divine Appointment

After a bite to eat and a siesta in our room we venture out onto the streets again. It is still remarkably quiet. The city tourist book highlights a few blocks called *Bayramyeri*, "holiday area." It is within walking distance and we eventually find it. The area has recently undergone a renewal with some streets newly paved in handsome cobblestones. But ironically, on this holy day, it doesn't feel much like a holiday area with all the shops closed up and hardly a soul in the place. On the way back we pass a blacksmith shop that is, unexpectedly, a hive of activity with two forges blazing. Then we realize they are cooking meat. The neighbours have pressed them into a BBQ operation and the bags of meat are lined up.

We guess, correctly, that there will always be refreshments at the *oto gar*. We have a glass of tea and a *simit*. This must be one place that never really shuts down, even during Korban Bayramı. Surprisingly, even here at this transportation hub, we still don't see any westerners. We are two Canadians in a strange land. And yet the Lord is near, and his people are near, as we have just discovered.

And perhaps there is a special reason the Lord has brought these two brothers into our lives on this particular day—to remind us we are not alone. This afternoon, as I check our email, I discover news from home. This morning, in his Prince

Edward Island home, my dad passed away. He was up early to make porridge for the household as was his practice. Then he made a pot of tea, English tea, not Turkish tea, definitely. Then having some severe heart pain he took the two morphine tablets that had been left out for him. Shortly after he called my sister for help. She called for an ambulance, but by 8:00 he had slipped away.

Dad turned 90 last August. He had been on borrowed time for a couple years, on palliative care, really. So this came as no great surprise. Yet death is always sooner than we think. I make the decision not to try to get back for the funeral. We had gone to Prince Edward Island in July and were present for Mom's passing. Since then I have kept in touch with dad by phone, the last time just days before we left on this trip. He would neither expect, not want us to break this journey. Our large family will gather round and take care of all that needs to be done. He would have enjoyed the story of our own divine appointment of earlier in the day.

Before the evening is over I have a phone call to make. This is to the contact number for the little Turkish house group we hope to meet up with tomorrow, Sunday. With my meager Turkish, talking to a stranger over the phone is a bit of a stretch, but I just have to go for it. I try to do most of the talking before he takes over and I lose the thread of the conversation. I find out that my contact is in Ankara, not Denizli, likely visiting family for the *bayram*. But the church will still gather, beginning at 11:00. He gives instructions on how to find the place and tells me to call him again if I need help. He ends with a word of blessing. I am sorry I will not get to meet him, at least not on this trip.

Colossians 1:21-23

Safely Home—Whole and Holy

. . . in order to present you holy and blameless and above reproach before him.

....

Glory to you Father
Bless you Jesus
Praise to you Holy Spirit.

How adventurous you are how imaginative!

You set in space this turquoise ball and populated it stepping back

to give us breathing space room to differentiate and choose you.

Or not.

Then, reckless love, you jumped in cross-deep to redeem us.

We would never in a month of Sabbaths come up with even the first word of this story line.

But you have already written the last word over dad (and over me too)
. . . GRACE.

Amen.

Why did Jesus, the Lamb of God, lay down his life?

Was it not, first of all, for the glory of God? In the first chapter of his letter to the Ephesians (a sister letter to this one) Paul has that infamous, eleven verse, single sentence, exclamation mark!— an eagle's eye perspective, eternity past to eternity future, on God's rescue mission. And it is shot through with attention to God's glory. In fact the entire passage is a kind of Jewish *berekah*—a prayer of blessing to God. The sacrificial death is more about God than us.

Yet it is also about us. For it is our salvation that brings glory to God. The death of Jesus unlocked the prison gates for us, released us from darkness and welcomed us into his kingdom light. Because of Jesus we have redemption, the forgiveness of sins. Because of Jesus we have a secure deposit of hope laid up in heaven for us (Colossians 1).

And furthermore, we *who once were alienated and hostile in mind, doing evil deeds, he has now reconciled in his body of flesh by his death, in order to present [us] holy and blameless and above reproach before him* (22).

Welcome home dad! What is it like to be presented holy and blameless before Holy God? Oh my! What an awesome and humbling, joyful and tearful moment of unspeakable thankfulness and more. Are you dancing for the first time?!

You were good, here on earth, but not that good, a pot cracked in places (you knew that). But you clung to Jesus, *giving thanks to the Father, who has qualified you to share in the inheritance of the saints in light* (12). My dad's a saint—wow!

Precious in the sight of the LORD
is the death of his saints.
Psalm 116:15

10. Sunday Worship in Denizli

Sunday morning we set out on the still strangely quiet streets of this normally bustling city. I estimate it will take us an hour to walk to the location of *Denizli Laodikya Kilisesi* (church) following another sketch map along unknown streets. The temperature is just perfect for the adventure. We check off the landmarks as we go—past the public hospital, past the park, past the waterless canal, past the area unmarked on Google that turns out (as suspected) to be a military base. We also pass a few street-side meat grinders helping the public (for a small fee) to make the most of the scraps after the main cuts have been claimed from their sacrifice offerings. We wonder if these are the same guys who offered their knife sharpening services on the same streets over the last couple of days. The sacrifice holiday has its very matter-of-fact and business-like side to it. But aside from these few practical reminders of what has just taken place, this is a beautiful city on a beautiful morning. We love the trees lining the streets and the grape vines running over trellises or up the sides of houses. The hedges are trimmed and the parks are well-kept and clean.

At last the end of our journey is in sight. Two more side-streets and we should find Sümbül street. Ah, there it is, it even has a sign. But how will we know when we come to the right building? We needn't have worried. There on the end of the building for all the world to see we read, "*Laodikya Kilisesi, AD 2012.*" And above this a cross with the words "Church of Jesus Christ" written beneath in Turkish. This is bold proclamation in an environment so often inhospitable to the followers of Jesus. For us it is a welcome sight.

We open the gate to the front yard and somewhere a dog barks. After a couple of minutes a woman's head appears on a balcony then disappears again. Then a man's head. Then we hear footsteps on the stairs and the door being unlocked. We briefly explain our presence and are greeted warmly. Turns out the service begins an hour later than the instructions we had received. But this is no problem and we are ushered inside to the meeting area on the ground floor. Our host turns out to be Farid, another Iranian believer. He is also a refugee in Turkey and is waiting for his Canadian papers to be processed so he can move to Edmonton. Imagine his surprise when two Canadians show up on his doorstep! Quickly come the glasses of tea to refresh us while we wait and look around.

We are impressed with the building. Typically a new group of believers in Turkey begins in rented space, or perhaps simply meets in someone's apartment. But landlords may not be happy about having Christians meeting in their facilities. The neighbours may complain. The police may be around more than is comfortable. So meeting places get shuffled around. This doesn't encourage stability in the fragile new congregation. But, if the momentum is there, and the finances are available, the push comes to purchase a building. Often, if not always, the bulk of the funds come from outside the country. Though, even if the money is available, it may still be hard to get a suitable building, and depending on the region of the country, getting permission to use the building as a meeting place may also be a challenge. But Christians remember that "The king's heart is a stream of water in the hand of the Lord; he turns it wherever he will" (Proverbs 21:1). After much prayer a place will be found, and permission to meet granted.

Here in Denizli these Christians have been able to purchase a whole building, reasonably new, with three floors above ground and a usable basement. Originally designed as three, roomy, self-contained apartments stacked on top of each other, the ground level has had most of the walls opened up so as to make a good-sized, though odd-shaped meeting area that can seat perhaps 80 people. This sanctuary is beautifully decorated. Front and centre is the communion table. There is also a large wall-mounted video screen with an overhead projector. Farid and his wife and daughter live on the floor above, with his parents who have just arrived from Iran. The small apartment on the top floor is used by the pastor when he is in town.

Farid no doubt has things to do before the service begins, but he takes time to talk with us and make us feel at home. He speaks no English, but fortunately is fluent in Turkish. Of course his mother tongue is Farsi. Gradually a few more people show up. They all greet us warmly. One man is from Bulgaria A woman comes with her Turkish mother, her father was Greek. But most seem to be Iranian. One man, Shamil, speaks good English, but no Turkish. We try to speak Turkish which includes most of the group, with occasional translation into English or Farsi for his sake. About a dozen people are present today. This is a good sized congregation for Turkey, but looks small in these generous facilities. Farid assures us that when the pastor is present the group is much larger.

It turns out this church is an off-shoot of a church in Ankara and today we will catch the sermon via live video feed over the internet. The singing is also led via video feed. It feels strange in this "high touch" culture to experience "high tech" worship. We feel more like spectators than participants as we stare at the images dancing on the wall. But we do have Communion together (that cannot be done at a distance!) And after the service we pray together.

There hadn't been much Scripture reading in the service that I could catch. So as we sit around a table I am bold enough to read some Scripture verses from Philippians in Turkish and share a few words of encouragement.

> *I thank my God in all my remembrance of you, always in every prayer of mine for you all making my prayer with joy, because of your partnership in the gospel from the first day until now. And I am sure of this, that he who began a good work in you will bring it to completion at the day of Jesus Christ (Phil. 1:3-6).*

I also mention that my dad passed away yesterday and read verse 21 from the same chapter: "For to me to live is Christ, and to die is gain." I tell them dad would echo those words. I am also aware that death is always close by for these refugees. I hope these words are also encouraging for them. They pray for us, as we pray for them. They seem pleased with their Canadian visitors.

Colossians 1:24-2:3

For I want you to know how great a struggle I have for you and for those at Laodicea and for all who have not seen me.

....

*Lord Jesus,
with what passion
you prayed in that garden.*

*In truth
you were pleading for me
for my deliverance.*

Blood, sweat, and tears.

*Forgive me Lord for my
low-cost prayers
if I pray at all.*

*Stir within me the pulse of
the Olympic athlete,
agonizing through
the "wall"
for the sake of a wreath.*

*Lord, in your mercy,
will you comfort the
church in Denizli,
will you knit them close,
will you grant them
a 20/20 vision of Jesus.*

*I pray through
the blood,
Amen.*

Four-Wheel-Drive Prayers

Again we see how Paul loves his granddaughter churches. And we who have grandchildren can understand this. Never a day goes by when we do not pray for them, each by name.

What are Paul's dreams for the church in Colossae, and for the sister churches of the Lycus Valley? Verse 2 of this chapter spells some of this out. Firstly, "that their hearts may be encouraged." Paul knows how easy it is to be dis-couraged (after weary months in jail, for example) and he longs to comfort them in their challenging environment.

Secondly, that they may be "knit together in love." How wonderful it is to be part of a close community. It is Christ who has made us one. How quickly we forgive any wrong, for Christ has forgiven me. This warm fellowship is itself a source of encouragement in tough times.

Thirdly, that they may "reach all the riches of full assurance of understanding and the knowledge of God's mystery, which is Christ." God's great secret is now out in the open—it is Jesus Christ. He is the door, the way, the centre-point of true faith. Paul longs for them to experience the riches of knowing this more deeply.

And back in verse 1 we see the depth of Paul's passion for them, his "great struggle." The word "struggle" is the Greek *agon*, from which we get the English words "agony," and "agonize." How does Paul agonize over them? Surely it is in prayer. We see this later in his reference to Epaphras "always *struggling* ["agonizing"] on your behalf in his prayers" (4:12). The same vocabulary is used of Jesus in his Gethsemane pleading (Luke 22:44).

How deep is our love for believers we are separated from?—or perhaps have not even met? Am I able to agonize for the Turkish church?

11. Over Lunch

The time has come to go, but as we get up to begin our goodbyes we are compelled to stay a little longer. We soon see why when the announcement comes that lunch is ready and we are invited to follow Farid upstairs to his apartment. Leaving our shoes outside the door we walk in to find a bright and pleasant home decorated with lovely carpets, Turkish of course. First we are invited to sit in the living room and some fruit is brought to us, pears, crisp and sweet, with a knife on each plate. We know well enough not to eat too much, there is more to come. Of course conversation continues through all this, Turkish with a mix of English and Farsi thrown in. If I can't think of a word I ask Shamil in English, who asks Farid in Farsi, who then speaks to me in Turkish!

One thing surprises us. They all speak of how wonderful it is to have such freedom to worship openly in Turkey. Back in Iran everything is so tightly regulated, and Christians especially, are constantly watched. They talk about friends and pastors who have been imprisoned, held in solitary confinement, tortured and even killed. They are so thankful to Turkey for providing a haven where they can worship freely and come and go as they please. Coming from Canada we are not sure Turkey is such an open a place for Christians. But we are learning that freedom is relative.

At one point Shamil asks me what I think about William M. Branham. Apparently this American Pentecostal preacher from earlier days (1909 – 1965) has quite a following in the Iranian church. Back in the day this name would have been widely recognized around North America, but alas I was born too late. I later discover that Branham became a very popular preacher in his time and had an extensive itinerant ministry that included dramatic healings as well as conversions. His ministry style—tent meetings, large "crusades," etc.—had a large influence on the development of the Pentecostal and later Charismatic movements. In his teaching, however, he strayed from orthodox Christian faith in a number of areas. He denied the doctrine of the Trinity and held to a "Jesus only" belief. He believed he was a reincarnation of Elijah the prophet, come to herald the return of the Lord. He also had odd interpretations of what happened in the Garden of Eden that led him to an extremely low view of women. But this I have learned about Mr. Branham since returning to Canada.

I ask Shamil to tell me what troubles him about this man. His main concern is Branham's claim to secret information received through visions. All I can say is that this makes me uneasy also. I tell Shamil about my recent studies in Colossians in preparation for this trip to the neighbourhood of old Colossae. One of the great themes of this letter is Paul's insistence that the Gospel of Jesus is *public* knowledge. He urges the church in Colossae not to be intimidated by super-spiritual types claiming to have insider information. He calls them to hold fast to the basic message brought by Epaphras, which is the same public message that is being heard "all over the world" (Col. 1:3-8). This point is reiterated in chapter two:

Therefore, as you received Christ Jesus the Lord, so walk in him, rooted and built up in him and established in the faith, just as you were taught, abounding in thanksgiving (Col. 2:6-7).

Paul is obviously concerned that the ordinary Christians in Colossae are being made to feel like second-class believers because they do not accept the teachings of these false teachers troubling the church there. Like Branham, these teachers in Colossae also called on their followers to follow restrictive rules of behaviour—a step backwards from the pathway of grace to the pathway of works. Paul, in his authority as God's apostle, gives the believers in Colossae permission to reject the negative judgment of these renegade teachers and to rejoice in the freedom found in Christ (Col. 2:16f.)

How unfortunate that in our day a similarly distorted form of the Christian faith has been exported to Iran. But we remember that satan has no imagination and "new" heresies are simply old heresies with a fresh coat of paint. God, in his written word, has given us the guidance and teaching to inoculate us against these viruses if we will attend to his word. Some of all this I try to share with my brother Shamil.

Meanwhile, since two Canadians have just walked through his door, Farid takes the opportunity to ask lots of questions about his future homeland, about the work situation, about the weather, about the country in general. He is surprised that the Canadian government doesn't support churches financially and asks about this a number of times. I tell him that though we have much freedom to worship, Canada is a secular country. I try to explain the concept of separation of church and state. This is a difficult notion for him to grasp.

We emphasize also that Farid needs to get on with learning English. Perhaps his friend Shamil can teach him English in return for Turkish lessons. The grandparents, too, are part of the conversation. Betty shows her grandchildren pictures to the delight of everyone.

Now we are called in to sit around the dining room table for a lunch of chicken and very fresh bread. The chicken is brought in freshly roasted from a nearby store (where did they find a place that is open on this second day of the *bayram*?) The bread is warm from the bakery. To this simple meal are added a few Iranian condiments. We sip on some fresh *ayran*. Great food, great company—what more would we want? Well, perhaps another glass of tea. We are ushered back to our soft seats and more tea is produced—Iranian tea we are assured.

These folk love their birth-country. If conditions ease they will go back in a flash. We sense they are only parked in Turkey. Their longings are backwards for their old life in Iran, and forwards towards the bright new life, as they hope, that waits for them in Canada. I try to encourage them to see themselves as missionaries to Turkey, sent by God. But their hearts are not in it. Yes there is a church in Denizli, but it seems the impact on the people who live here is small as yet. So it is good to remember what Jesus said about such a small amount of yeast leavening a bowlful of flour (Matthew 13:33).

How we enjoy our fellowship. As we get up to go, for the third or fourth time, we exchange email addresses and take photos. After protracted good byes we set off once again for the hotel, down hill all the way this time. We barely have to glance at our map. What a day. Thank you Lord!

Colossians 2:4-13   Inoculate Us Against Delusion

that no one may delude you with plausible arguments.
....

Heavenly Father, do you get nervous when you see me leaving the house?

How easily I am seduced so soon forgetting my incomparable Christ.

Thank you for leading me back to these words.

Thank you for holding my nose to the page until the words come into focus in my slow heart and I am anchored again in Jesus.

But there is more. I confess my own tongue needs tethering.

Let me not slip into my own fast-talk smoothing others down parallel paths to Destruction.

I pray in the name of the Living Truth, Amen

A few years ago a English businessman was driving along a country lane in Yorkshire. He was religiously following the instructions of his GPS device, no doubt having selected beforehand the most soothing voice option. He did not discover he was being led astray until he smashed his BMW through a gate and came to a stop dangling over a cliff.

Paul, chained up in that dark prison cell, has received news that the church in Colossae is being led astray. How sweet are the voices of these dodgy preachers, and how persuasive their rhetoric. But they are not tracking with the Gospel of Jesus Christ. And the end of their road is destruction.

What can Paul do to defend his dear ones? He is chained down in a prison cell. But he can send them a letter. And so we see the power of words, inspired by the Holy Spirit of God.

First he calls a spade a spade. These smooth talkers are trying to deceive you (2:4). They are trying to take you captive (2:8).

Second he reminds the church of what they have heard from the beginning. The idea of a Messiah may have been murky and mysterious in the past, but now it is public knowledge—Epaphras has already taught them about Jesus (1:7). So keep walking in the same direction (2:6).

Third he reminds them of their intimate relationship with Jesus, portrayed, especially, in their baptism. They have been buried with Christ in baptism, and also raised with Christ, "made alive together with him" (2:12-13)—it doesn't get any better than this!

How can Paul street-proof these brothers and sisters in Colossae?—by reminding them of the Gospel they already know, and by refocusing their hearts on Jesus.

12. Next Stop, Adana

Monday morning we are up at the crack of sparrows—we have a plane to catch. Çardak Airport is 60kms out of town and our flight is early. Last night we arranged for the shuttle bus to pick us up. Now it is 6:20 a.m. and the *kapitan* is right on time. We pay our 10 liras each for the pleasant drive through open country to the airport.

We are not the only ones up early. We see tractors out in the fields, farmers getting an early start on their fall ploughing. Part of the journey we travel alongside a new, or possibly renewed, rail line. This puzzles me since I thought Denizli was the end of the line from Izmir. I later discover there are no passenger trains using this line at present. The *Pamukkale Express* which used to whisk passengers from Istanbul to Denizli was suspended in 2008, possibly due to the construction of the new high-speed rail network. No word yet on when, or if, the old train service will resume. We'll have to check into this for our next visit.

Yes, we wonder if there will be another visit. Just as we still wonder at the meaning of this present visit. How does the Lord feel about our strange desire to travel all this way just to be his representatives in this city for a few days? We trust that he is pleased, and that from heaven's perspective our escapade makes sense.

Denizli airport is small and we pass quickly through check in and security. But we skip breakfast, the food is ridiculously expensive here. We board the plane and after a one hour flight land in Istanbul's Asian-side airport, Sabiha Gökçen Havalimanı. It is named after one of Atatürk's adopted daughters. This woman, at the age of 23, and at the encouragement of her father, became the world's first female fighter pilot, the beginning of a remarkable career in aviation.

Our day of air travel is much more mundane. We sit through the weary hours waiting for our connection to Adana. Direct flights are manageable, but a day spent hanging around airplanes and airports is a lost day in my humble opinion. It might be better to take a bus/train combo next time. At least with surface travel you get to see the country.

But eventually we do arrive in Adana and walk off the plane into very familiar surroundings. This city was once our home for a year and a half. On other occasions we have walked out to the main road to catch a bus. This time we are not traveling as light and so splurge on a taxi and travel in comfort to our destination. I have booked a night in a nice hotel along the river—a little reward for Betty (and me) for enduring our less than ideal digs in Denizli. Courtesy of internet booking we got a great deal on the room rate.

The Bosnali Otel is a beautifully renovated historic building. Exposed posts and beams preserve some of the ambience of days gone by. In our room we find fresh local mandarin oranges set out for us. We reach out through the window to open the old-fashioned shutters and there, through the palm trees, is a lovely view of the Seyhan river.

After getting our belongings sorted we climb up to the roof-top terrace for an even better view of our surroundings. To the left is the massive Merkez Mosque rivalling the famous Blue Mosque in size and ornamentation, but only 20 years old. We marvel at all the new construction across on the east side of the river. We can see a huge shopping mall and some large condominium developments, all serviced by the new metro system. This was a pretty run-down area when we lived here, not a place we felt safe exploring. How this has changed. Then, to our right is the Taş Köprüsü (Stone Bridge) dating from about AD380. It was used by motorized vehicles up until 2007 and is now reserved for pedestrians. At 310 meters in length, with 21 arches, it remains an impressive work of engineering.

The Seyhan river is one of the longest rivers in Turkey carrying the melted snow and rain from the Taurus mountains down across the fertile Çurkurova plain and out to the Mediterranean coast. In earlier times the river flooded annually, to the misery of the inhabitants of the region (though to the benefit of the soil.) But in the last century the river was tamed by a series of dams allowing for both hydro-electric power generation and for controlled irrigation. During the summer the great river becomes little more than a trickle as water is fed off across the city through four huge irrigation canals, later to be distributed through a web of lesser canals. But now, in mid-October, the river is high and the canals almost empty. No wonder the Romans put up this stone bridge. Any army traveling east or west would have struggled to cross this barrier.

Unfortunately the bridge was built too late to be of any benefit to Barnabas as he left Antioch to seek out Paul in his hometown some 60 kms west of here (see Acts 11:22-26). If he took the overland route he would have crossed this river somewhere near here. But perhaps he found a boat that would take him across the northeast corner of the Mediterranean directly to Tarsus. The Bible story is never far from our hearts in this part of the world.

> *²² The report of this came to the ears of the church in Jerusalem, and they sent Barnabas to Antioch. ²³ When he came and saw the grace of God, he was glad, and he exhorted them all to remain faithful to the Lord with steadfast purpose, ²⁴ for he was a good man, full of the Holy Spirit and of faith. And a great many people were added to the Lord. ²⁵ So Barnabas went to Tarsus to look for Saul, ²⁶ and when he had found him, he brought him to Antioch. For a whole year they met with the church and taught a great many people. And in Antioch the disciples were first called Christians.*

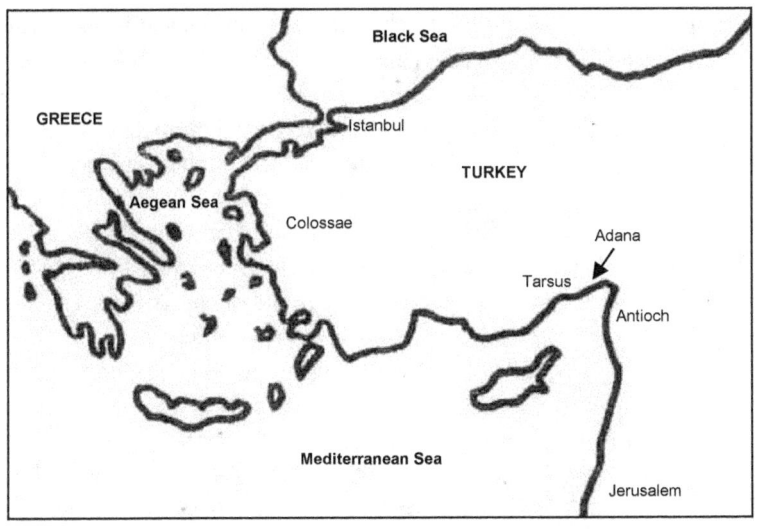

Colossians 2:13-14   Dept Free! Dept Free!

*And you,
who were dead
... God made alive
together with him,
having forgiven us
all our trespasses,
by cancelling the
record of debt
... this he set aside
nailing it to the cross.*

....

*Heavenly Father,
forgive me for tinkering
with my indebtedness.*

*As though it could be
wiped clean with some
sort of soft secular soap
(or even the blood of
another solemn sheep.)*

*Would you have laid
down your only Begotten
if there had been any
other way?*

*With your own hand
you hammered the nails.*

*Then three days cold
you took Him up again
and me alongside him
to life, to LIFE!*

*Give me words to tell of
such release, O Lord.*

Amen.

Do you remember the before and after photos in the so-called infomercials?—before and after he had hair implants... before and after she tried the anti-aging cream... The *before* pictures are grainy black and whites; the *after* pictures are rich in colour, beautifully photo-shopped. The desirability of the *after* is dramatically enhanced against the miserable backdrop of the *before*.

Once again, Paul contrasts our *before* and *after*. How dead we were in our sins. We were lost. No hope, no future, far beyond self-help. We were dead. As dead as Jesus in that stone cold tomb. As dead as a man can be.

But God—and God is the subject of all the verbs in this section—but God "made us alive together with Christ." Just as Christ shared in our death, so we share in his life. If Christ is not alive, if he is still in the ground somewhere, we are still hopeless, futureless, and hell-bound. But Christ lives—absolutely! awesomely! majestically! powerfully! joyfully! eternally! And God has made us to share in his resurrection life.

"Having forgiven us all our trespasses . . ." Can we be alive in Christ and not be forgiven?—impossible! But we are forgiven, and not just partially, not just from what we might consider little sins, but "all." The Greek word for "forgive" in this sentence is a compound of *charis*, "grace." Our sins have been blown away by grace!

Paul spells this out further . . . God has cancelled (blotted out, irrecoverably erased) the (handwritten) record of indebtedness against us. CIA's best techies cannot recover these files. For God has personally taken them up and nailed them to the cross. My debt-notice nailed above, not a sheep, but my Lord. Paid in full! Paid in full!

13. Visiting a Dear Friend

But we have not come to Adana to admire the view, at least not primarily. We have come to visit friends. And first on our list is our dear friend Yakub. After sitting in airports and on planes most of the day we decide to walk the couple of kilometres to Yakub's home. And so we set out across more-or-less familiar streets. There have been some changes since we lived here and a couple of times we have to detour.

At about the half-way point we are ready for a rest, and a bite to eat. We each order *tavuk döner durum* from little sidewalk eatery. Slices of chicken are shaved off the vertical spit and tucked into half a loaf of fresh bread, along with salad, sauce, etc. making a substantial and delicious sandwich. While we wait we are seated front and centre on the sidewalk. We are used to being thus displayed. If the foreigners eat here, the food must be good. We have become advertising! But we do enjoy our meal and get up satisfied. The bill?—five dollars including two glasses of *ayran* and the tip.

We continue up Atatürk street towards the train station. When we lived here we moved into an apartment on the north side of the station and Yakub was our neighbour. Expecting a long detour east or west to one of the bridges over the tracks, we discover a new underpass that thankfully shortens our path. And so we approach the street-side stand, a hut really, ten feet by six feet, from which Yakub sells his refreshments. The location is doubly convenient, for not only does it sit at the end of his garden, making his commute a breeze, it is also directly across the road from the *Borsa Lisesi*, Borsa high school and its ever hungry inmates.

We walk cautiously up to his stand feeling a little uncomfortable about surprising him like this. But what can we do? He has no internet. A letter would not get to him. Will he still be there? Will he be in good health? (or even alive?) But we need not have worried. There he is. His face lights up when he spots us and he throws his hands in the air. We can see he is delighted at the sudden appearance of his Canadian friends. He calls us in through the garden gate and rushes over to greet us. A bear hug and a kiss on each cheek for me, a more modest greeting for Betty. He calls to the house and quickly his wife appears. Now it is Betty's turn for the hugs and kisses. We are invited to take a seat outside under the shade of a trellis covered by a grape vine. He planted that vine when we still lived next door. In six years it has grown to produce a thick leafy canopy—nature's aircon in these parts.

Yakub is the same age as me, though his rough and ready environment has aged him more. He began life in a humble village some distance from the city of Adana. He had three years in the village school but learned little, so he told me. Later he taught himself to read. When the time came he did his *askerlik*, his obligatory two years of military service. He was posted on the border with Georgia in the far north east of Turkey, likely his first taste of travel beyond his home province. After that he got a job with the railway, track maintenance I think, where he remained until retirement.

Most Turkish men continue with some kind of work even after they officially retire. Partly because they need to get out of the house and keep busy with something (retirement age comes early in Turkey) and partly because pensions are low and they need some kind of supplementary income. Jakub's plan was to make and sell *şalgam*, a vinegary drink made from purple carrots. *Şalgam* is a popular thirst-quencher of the region, much loved for its tangy taste and rich colour. It is also thought to have health benefits. When someone tells you he is from Adana, ask him if he likes *şalgam*. If his eyes light up you know he is telling the truth! I like it too, though it is an acquired taste (Betty refuses to touch it!) Jakub produces his *şalgam* using only traditional methods and people drive across town to buy his artisan product.

So Jakub looks out across the rough counter of his humble store and observes the world with curious and intelligent eyes. Eight years earlier he had watched as two foreigners moved in to the sixth floor of the apartment building next door. Who were they? Where did they come from? It wasn't long before he caught my eye, and so began our friendship.

Jakub is self educated and always wanting to learn more about the world. I became his window on Canada and he asked many questions. I would watch him sit back with his eyes half closed trying to imagine what life is like in that strange and distant land. Jakub is also a natural born teacher. He speaks no English, of course, so he has to do his best with my limited Turkish. He peers at me intently as I try to express some knew thought. "Just give me an *ip*," he pleads in frustration, just a little *thread*. Then suddenly the light bulb comes on and he raises his hand. "This is how we say that," or "Here is the word we use," he tells me, then laughs with satisfaction. He does not believe in reincarnation, but he does say if he had a second chance he would be a teacher. He already is my teacher.

Yakub laughs a lot. He is fun to be with. In the evenings his friends gather round under the grape vine. I am surprised by the wide range of social and economic background of those who come. From Yusuf, a poor neighbour, now unable to speak because of a stroke (but his mind is still bright, Jakub is quick to remind me), to former workmates, to a retired banker who enjoys the company and wit of my village friend. When the conversation gets too much for me and I am clearly out of the loop Jakub calls a time out. "I have to translate for John," he laughs. Then, in his folksy way, using dramatic sign language and simplified Turkish, he gets me up to speed.

Jakub and his wife seem especially happy as we sit in the shade, sipping tea and catching up with the news. And we soon learn the reason why. Around the corner of the house comes their older daughter with a baby on her arm—their first grandchild, a girl! We are delighted too. We know the joy of grandchildren. We take turns holding the little bundle before Jakub claims her for his own. This is a trans-cultural moment.

At one point we look up and there is our old *kapıcı*, the custodian from the apartment building next door. His son and daughter are with him. How they have grown since we first met them. They are glad to see us, and we to see them. It's like old home week! Before moving away from Adana we ate our last meal in the home of this family, sitting (somewhat awkwardly) on the floor around a delicious spread of very traditional Turkish food. It is good to see them again.

By way of filling us in on the recent news, Jakub tells us that a few days earlier he and my *kapıcı* had purchased a sheep together and sacrificed it in the little garden just behind where we are sitting. Neither of them are well off, but by sharing the cost they can fulfill their religious obligations.

Then Jakub is silent for a moment, observing us. I realise he is suddenly looking at his sacrifice ritual through the eyes of these foreigners. What does all this look like to them? Do they think it is crude and uncivilized? I admire his ability to step into another person's shoes and look at himself from a new angle. "Do people celebrate *Korban Bayramı* in Canada," he asks me. "Some do," I tell him, "but very few." "Why so few?" he asks. I notice his wife listening intently.

They already know we are Christians. It didn't take long for us to get to the point where we could talk openly about that. A little later I had the privilege of giving him a Bible in Turkish. He received it with great interest and, between customers, began reading it seriously, reporting to his family what he was discovering there. I also gave him some other Christian literature. He was clearly open, but not yet near the point of conversion, as far as I could tell. Not long after that we moved away from the city, then returned to Canada. Now this wonderful opening to speak directly of Christ once again.

I tell him that although not everyone in Canada is a Christian, our country has been greatly influenced by the Christian faith. Then I explain that we Christians do have a blood sacrifice. But our sacrifice was fulfilled 2000 years ago. Our sacrifice is Jesus, the Son of God, who gave up his life for our sin. So because Jesus was willing to sacrifice his own life, we no longer need to offer our own sacrifices year after year.

They both listen quietly, occasionally nodding their heads. I wish my Turkish was better, but I think they understand the heart of what I am trying to say. It is a special moment. We pray that the Spirit will bring lasting fruit out of this conversation. How we long for them to come to a saving knowledge of Jesus. We really want to spend eternity with these friends.

Then the moment passes. More visitors arrive, this time relatives from Tarsus, hometown of Jakub's wife. We stand for the greetings and begin our farewells. It is three hours since we first arrived and time enough to go. But we assure them we will see them again before we leave town. Jakub points out a good place to catch a minibus that will get us close to the hotel. We head off down the street in yet another overcrowded bus. Peering through the windows into the darkness of an unfamiliar part of town we hope we are heading in the right direction. But eventually we see the famous Stone Bridge. We hop off and walk the short distance to our room. What a day!

Colossians 2:15 Devils Declawed

He disarmed the rulers and authorities and put them to open shame, by triumphing over them in him.

....

*Heavenly Father
you have set me
free indeed!*

Whom shall I fear?!

*For his kindness
and his grace
even to me
dark hordes of heaven
tried to shame your
One and Only.*

*But (hallelujah!)
he shamed them
leaving them starkly
naked.*

*Whom then shall I fear
in this wide, wide world?!
For you are with me
rod and staff comforting.*

*Who will separate us
from your love O Lord?
—mocker? murderer?*

*Thank you Lord Jesus
for gathering us up
and sending us out
under your victory banner,
Amen*

We asked one Turkish couple how they met Jesus. Their answer surprised us. "We were desperate for deliverance," they said. They had been caught up in so-called "Folk Islam" which incorporates superstition, the use of magic rituals, spells, charms and other occult practices. Instead of being delivered from their fears, as they had hoped, they sank into deeper and deeper bondage to dark spiritual forces. At last they discovered Jesus Christ. He alone could set them free from the grip of satan.

Here in Colossians 2:15 Paul paints a dramatic word-picture of the declawing of the devil and his minions. God, through Christ, *disarmed* them. But our English translations don't capture the full force of the word. Paul uses an intensified form of the verb—they are *aggressively stripped off*! There is no question about the outcome. These *rulers and authorities* are slammed against the wall, cuffed and stripped of their weapons.

But that is not all. Then they are led on a "walk of shame." Paul uses the idea of a Roman *triumph*. This was the victory march through the streets of Rome, as a general led his humiliated captives before the festive crowds. There was no doubt as to who was the victor and who were the vanquished.

Again, we marvel at the sanctified imagination of Paul, who in that grim prison cell can see with the eye of faith beyond the stone walls and the locked doors, to the resounding victory of Christ. At the cross we were not only delivered from sin, but also torn free from the grip of the devil.

Is satan still active? of course he is. He "prowls around like a roaring lion," writes Peter to the earlier inhabitants of the land of Turkey (1 Peter 5:8). But he is a declawed lion, he is a dog on a leash. He is no threat to those who are watchful.

14. Tuesday

After a good night's rest in our pleasant hotel room we make our way down for breakfast. There is no buffet. Instead, the food is brought in style to our table, lots of food, including a very fine omelette. Across from us a couple enjoy their own breakfast while their free-range toddler explores the room. When the happy little fellow comes to visit us, his parents rush over and apologize. We tell them we are used to children (and grandchildren) and we enjoy his cheery visit. Besides, he has opened up the conversation. We discover this Turkish family is visiting from Germany. They have driven here to spend six weeks traveling around the country. The father works for a paper manufacturing company. They seem well educated and well off. They have not lost their Turkish friendliness.

After breakfast Betty and I go for a walk along the riverfront. It is very beautiful and I snap some photos trying to preserve the moment. The water level is higher than we remember seeing it, possibly because at this time of year not much is being drawn off for irrigation. Later we see one of the main irrigation feeder canals that crosses the city. It carries only a trickle. Soon the canals will be completely dry for the winter months—great places for kids to play soccer. Today the beauty of the river is somewhat diminished by plastic shopping bags along the edge and floating in the water. But the old bridge is still as impressive, and the huge, six-minaret mosque also. I find an angle that gives me a shot of the mosque reflected in the still water.

We see a local entrepreneur out on the river in his little rowboat. He is setting up a string of colourful balloons a hundred feet offshore. Then he will sit on the bank and wait for customers. For a modest fee aspiring sharp-shooters get to use his air rifle and show off their skills. I capture all the balloons in one shot, but my hunting is done only with a camera.

Over the past few years a large area alongside the river has been cleared of ramshackle structures and messy commercial enterprises. The resulting green space has been beautifully landscaped. Many of the historic buildings have been renovated. This neighbourhood is worth exploring further, but it is time for us to move on. Besides, the sun is already uncomfortably hot. We head back to the hotel in search of shade, and to check out. We will leave the suitcases in the lobby until later in the day. Now we have more friends to visit.

Taking our bearings from the river we set out inland, walking in the shade where we can, looking for Saydam street. Here is the workplace of Selim *amca* (uncle Selim)—a dear brother in Christ. A little further along the street is his home. When we lived here it was in his workplace that I had my thrice weekly Turkish lessons with Hamit *hoca* (teacher Hamit), also a believer. So these streets became familiar to me and I got to know a few other people along the way also.

At the end of Saydam street I think it wise to call ahead. Selim is a little older than I am and I wonder about his heart. It might not be good to just walk in on him. I try his workplace number and discover it has been changed. Well, it is over six years since we lived around here. I try his home number and get Birsen, Selim's wife. She soon figures out who I am and is delighted to hear that Betty and I are in town. Because of the holiday Selim is not in his office today. They invite us to their house. Since I'm no longer sure of the way Selim will come to meet us.

On the street we pass the barber shop owned by the father of a young Turkish man who had moved to Canada. After we returned to live again in Canada we miraculously ran into him in Toronto. Father is not in today but I pass along the news that his son is doing well. I had phoned the son from Vancouver before we left.

We see Selim before he sees us and watch as his face lights up. We are warmly greeted, I with a bear hug and bristly cheek kisses, Betty with a little more reserve. He leads us triumphantly down the sidewalk Betty on one arm, me on the other, cutting a swath through the busy foot traffic. A few blocks further and we dodge into a side alley, then left again, coming to the entrance to his apartment building. Selim unlocks the door and in we go. We squeeze into the tiny elevator and slowly climb to the third floor.

Here we are! The door to their suite is open and slippers are waiting for us. We politely take our shoes off outside, but Birsen quickly brings them in. Because of the *bayram* most of the family is home and we are glad to see them all. My, how the younger ones have grown since we left. One daughter is married and lives in Sweden now, unable to make the trip home this year. Another daughter is teaching in Mardin but is back for the holidays. The youngest daughter is beginning university in a town a couple of hours away. She will head back this afternoon. One son is home, the other working. What a great reunion.

Birsen brings in the coffee. Making Turkish coffee is a fine art, but she has a reputation for being the best. The tops of the little cups are all covered in foam, the sign of a pro. Alongside is the traditional glass of water. Tea is far more common in Turkey and we will get our tea later, but coffee served this way is the traditional welcome for honoured guests.

It is good to see them and to catch up with their news, even though our heads are spinning from the effort of communicating in Turkish. Selim has a strong accent and I often need the help of the children. We talk about the church he belongs to. They have moved to a new location, still renting. But the congregation is growing and new people are coming. Their long-time missionary pastor is a faithful shepherd. We hope to join them for the worship on Sunday afternoon. In a lull in the conversation I bravely read a passage of Scripture. It is received with appreciation. I once saw Selim's Bible in his office. It has more underlining and highlighting than any Bible I have ever seen.

Birsen insists we stay for a "little lunch" and disappears into the kitchen. Betty follows her. Of course the spread that appears is lavish. Birsen's cooking is as accomplished as her coffee-making. We can't really do justice to the meal, but we do our best. This is Turkish hospitality.

And then it is time to go. Some of their family members have buses to catch. And we want to check in at our American friends' home where we will stay the rest of our time in Adana. More goodbyes, then a twenty-minute walk back to the hotel for our luggage. At one point I suddenly hear someone call my name. It is one of my old street friends. He has remembered me. There he is, just as he has been for many years now, tending his large hand cart, a kind of mobile hardware store. More cheek kisses and greetings. Betty buys some shoe polish from him. We have to twist his arm to accept money for it. Remember this man Lord, who remembers us so kindly.

There is time for one more little detour. We duck into a rambling, covered shopping area, a kind of poor man's Grand Bazaar (of Istanbul fame). It is a real rabbit warren of alleyways and passages. Hamit once introduced me to a friend of his here. After that I visited him often, but now I can't seem to find my way. Oh well, no shame in asking for directions. I interrupt three bearded gents deep in conversation. One of them kindly leads me to Arif's little shop.

Sure enough, there he is. Arif smiles with recognition as we thank our guide and step inside. He sells mostly tea, much of it in bulk. But he also has bulk instant coffee and bulk coffee whitener, plus spices and some other odds and ends that don't always seem to fit together, like bottles of perfume, for example. And small it is, this shop, under eight feet square with barely room to sit on a couple of stools amid the piled cartons.

Arif calls down a passage and three glasses of steaming tea are promptly delivered. They come with the local complement of no less than three sugar cubes resting on each saucer. Since none present uses that much sugar Arif carefully places the leftovers in a jar to be taken home when it is full—quite frequently I suspect.

Over tea we get updates on his wife and children, and in turn share our grandchildren photos. After a decent interval I ask Arif if he has been back to church. Apparently very rarely. I was told he was a "secret believer," but after I got to know him he was open to talking about the Christian faith. I used to give him Christian books to read while he sat and waited for customers. He appreciated that. I got him to church once, so he could meet other Turkish believers and participate in worship. But he remained very cautious about any public identification with Christianity. And we can sympathize with him, cornered as he is in this very tight working environment. If this little community ever turned against him his business would be over. And yet, does not Jesus call us to confess him openly? It is so easy for us to say these things.

Well, if Arif cannot go to church, the church can come to Arif. And so it has today. We have come to encourage him, and to remind him of Christ and his people. He is clearly happy to see us, and we trust our visit has been a blessing.

At the hotel we collect our luggage and take a taxi to the nearest metro station. Even though it is not far, the young driver doesn't seem to know where it is and I have to direct him to a place I have never seen either. It is all good Turkish practice, and all good-natured. The metro turns out to be free of charge because of the holidays. I take a couple of photos of the station before I realise the security guy across the tracks is shouting at me. I had not noticed the "no cameras" sign. Betty pretends she is not with me! It appears I will escape without jail time (crazy foreigner!) We wait only a few minutes before the next train comes along. We even get seats.

When we moved to Adana years earlier the metro was half-built and abandoned. The construction funds had run out (or possibly "run away.") For five years it had sat this way. Most people we talked to did not expect it would ever be completed. But then, to everyone's surprise, it was. It is a fine system, partly underground, sometimes overhead. We are impressed by the quality of the construction and the frequency of service. It has proven to be a great way to get across town avoiding the crowded streets. This is just one example of many long-unfinished infrastructure projects that have been brought to completion under the political stability of the last decade.

We get off at the end of the line after traveling from one end of Adana to the other. We take our time pulling our suitcases over the rough sidewalk as we make our way to our friend's house. When we first moved here we stayed in this house for a couple of months while they were away. So we know this area well too, although lots of new buildings have gone up since those days. It's a modern, growing part of town, very different from old Saydam street.

Since our friends' children have grown up and flown the nest they have some empty space on the top floor of their town house. They have generously offered to let us stay with them during the rest of our time here. Most days we will just have breakfast together, spending the rest of the time out and about, but today we are invited for dinner.

More warm greetings. We are glad to see these faithful servants of the Lord who have lived here for many years. We hand over the treasured Canadian maple syrup, as promised. (A small bribe towards the use of their home.) No bristly cheek kisses here, by the way, and no leaving shoes outside the door. Now we do our best to adjust now to American culture.

Colossians 2:16-23   Shame-Proofing the Church

Let no one disqualify you, insisting on asceticism and worship of angels, going on in detail about visions, puffed up without reason . . . and not holding fast to the Head
. . . .

Heavenly Father,
my glory,
and the lifter of my head,
I praise you.

If I had to stand on
my abstinences and
my observances
I would sink in shame.

But you,
in your amazing grace,
have set my feet
on the true Rock
which is Christ.

And they who point
shame to me,
find themselves pointing
to Jesus, O glory!

You buried my shame
in a far, forgotten place.

Then set me at your table,
a child of the King.
Amen!

Churches are places of healing and hope. They are communities of grace, havens of hospitality. Or are they? What happens when churches become toxic? What happens when pastors and teachers stray from holding fast to Christ and begin to pressure people into their own tight religious systems?

The closing verses of Colossians chapter two are notoriously difficult to interpret. And we remember again that reading Paul's letters is like listening to just one end of a telephone conversation. Without knowing what is happening at the other end it is not always easy to make sense of all the particulars. But the overall meaning does come through.

The troublesome teachers in Colossae are laying a "guilt trip" on the church—or, more accurately, a "shame trip"! You are not trying hard enough (they say). You are not fasting enough . . . You are not observant enough . . . Until you get serious about these religious practices you will never attain our level of spirituality (or share in our *visions*.)

But Paul, jealous for the health and joy of the church in Colossae pulls the rug from under these counterfeits. They have constructed their own spirituality out of a frothy mix of pseudo-Jewish asceticism and pagan obsessions. They are nothing but self-inflated windbags, he writes. They have confused the *shadows* of worldly religion for the *substance* which is Christ (17).

Bottom line?—do not listen to their so-called "judgments." They have absolutely no authority to "disqualify" you. Why?—because they have not held fast to the Head, who is Christ (19). True, in a sense they are right, we are not good enough. But their remedy is dead wrong. Let us place our hope in Christ alone, not in ramped up religion. It is he alone who nourishes us and knits us back together.

15. Soles and Souls

Betty decides to stay home and rest up this morning. It has been a heavy week. After devotions and breakfast, I head off downtown alone. Years earlier I had discovered a small tourist office that gave away nice maps of the city. The office has relocated and the new maps are not as useful—too much advertising!—but I take a couple. I think they are glad to see me, Adana doesn't get many tourists. History buffs find better pickings elsewhere, and the warm Mediterranean is fifty kilometres away.

Next I look around for a place to change money (I'm getting in lots of walking today) then off to the train station to buy tickets for our Sunday afternoon departure. We will take the overnight train to Ankara. It's a wonderful way to travel and for $40 each we get our own little room for the night as well as the trip. At the ticket office I speak in my clearest Turkish to the patient lady behind the glass. She gets me to right out my strange name on a piece of paper. I double check the tickets to make sure date, time and destination are correct. That was a stroke of luck!

With business out of the way it is time for pleasure. I have planned a visit to Kaan the cobbler. Kaan is a faithful follower of Christ. He and his good wife are active in one of the little churches here. To their sorrow (and the sorrow of their parents) they have not been able to have children.

Earlier I phoned John to make arrangements about visiting his workshop. Since I don't quite remember the location I will call him when I get close and he will talk me in. First I hike over to the nearest metro station and hitch a ride. Then I start walking in the general direction and dial up Kaan. To my surprise I get his wife. Seems my good friend forgot to take his cell phone to work this morning. Mrs. Kaan does her best to describe the route, but between my limited Turkish and lack of knowledge of the area I am getting nowhere. She is apologetic and I am a little frustrated. What can we do?

I look up the street and see an older woman coming down the sidewalk with her shopping in hand. What could go wrong? This is an open, public area. I stop her and ask for help, holding out my phone. Fortunately the woman quickly grasps the situation and is soon chattering away with Mrs. Kaan. Turns out I am not too far off track. I thank the woman for her help and head off in the right direction. She heads home with a bemused smile on her face and a story to tell about stray foreigners who break the rules and talk to a strange woman on the street!

How good it is to see Kaan again, he is a dear brother in Christ. He always has such a wonderful smile. I sit on an old chair and we talk as he continues to work. His hands are permanently stained from the dyes and polish. The shop smells of leather. His workbench is littered with the tools of his trade. I like this place.

As we talk, customers wander in. One holds out a pair of sandals and bargains over a small repair job. Another picks up some shoes that have been re-soled. A guy comes in with a broken pressure-cooker lid. Kaan rattles through a box of old hardware and finds a screw that will fix the trouble. It is hard to make a living at this kind of work—a couple of liras here and there.

But these customers get more than they bargained for. Because while he works Kaan prays to his Lord. He prays for customers who will be open to hearing the Gospel. And more often than the rules of mere coincidence allow, he is able to talk about his faith. His little workshop is a beacon of light in a dim world. How else will his customers ever hear about Jesus? But God has set a Christian cobbler in their midst!

I ask Kaan what he is reading these days. He is reading First Samuel. What am I reading?—Colossians. I am sad to hear he is not asked to do much preaching these days. In earlier times, when we still lived here, he would sometimes call me up late on Saturday evening. He was working on his sermon for the following day after a week of long, long hours in his shop. I would ask about his text and theme. It was a scramble to keep up in my limited Turkish. But I would try to offer some input, perhaps a parallel text he hadn't thought about, or a new angle. He still appreciates those Saturday night study sessions.

Throughout my visit an older man has been sitting quietly in the corner. Eventually I discover this is "uncle." Uncle had been living on the street. Kaan has been letting him sleep overnight in his workshop. After a while Uncle makes tea for us. Hot tea in this heat? But yes, it is refreshing. "Fight iron with iron," is the Turkish expression.

I have heard that, in recent years, Kaan has graduated from repairing shoes, to making shoes. Since I need new dress shoes I want to buy a pair from him. We pick out a pre-built pair from the shelf. Before he lets me take them he insists on carefully hand stitching around the perimeter of the sole. The soles had been glued on, but for me he will add stitching for extra strength. I put my new shoes on and find them soft and comfortable. As I pay for them he picks up the shoes I have been wearing. He wants to give them a tune-up. He will get them back to me when we meet in church on Sunday.

But now it is time for me to leave. I have arranged to meet up with Betty. She is attending a women's Turkish Bible study not too far from here. To my surprise Can says, "I'll drive you." This poor cobbler now owns a car? But it turns out he is a driver for a vehicle owned by his church. We jump in and it is only a short drive to the meeting place with Betty. Lord, remember Kaan and his wife.

Betty and I head out to the main street and wait for the next bus. We are now off to see Jakub and his wife again. As we hop off the bus and walk in his side street we meet him heading out on his bicycle. "Back soon," he calls to us. Daughter #2 is keeping an eye on his shop. By the time we reach his home he is back already. Betty is ushered inside to be with the women.

First, Jakub and I sit outside under the grape vine. It is nice and cool there in spite of the hot afternoon sun. But there are so many interruptions from customers that I offer to stay with him in his little shop. It is surely a Spirit led moment. For suddenly I see his Bible, the one I gave him years earlier, sitting on a shelf under the counter, wrapped in plastic for safe-keeping. I open it up and read from the place where John the

Baptist calls Jesus the Lamb of God (John 1). I link this to the conversation we had two days earlier about why Christians don't sacrifice a sheep each year. Jakub is interested and asks me to mark the place so he can read it again later. It takes very little to get him reading the Bible, he just needs encouraging.

Before long we get news that food has been prepared. We had been invited especially for a nice dinner. Jakub and I agree to eat outside while the women eat inside with proper table and chairs. It's not the best arrangement but he needs to keep and eye out for customers. Mrs. Jakub has cooked a number of dishes: beef and vegetables together, a lamb dish, rice done the Turkish way, salad, pickles, and dangerously hot peppers in a side dish. With all this, of course, comes the ever-present fresh bread (never eaten with butter). We drink water and şalgam, the tea will come later. I am surprised how little Jakub eats, although there is far more food in front of us than we can possibly consume. I guess this is how he keeps trim and healthy. I try to limit my intake, but I also want to show my appreciation of the great meal.

After our plates are cleared and the remainder of the food is taken away Betty and Mrs. Jakub and her daughters and the granddaughter come out to join us. We drink glasses of tea and nibble on a lovely custard desert (we would eat more but we are more than full).

How good it is to eat food together. In the past we have invited them to come and eat with us. I wonder if that will ever happen again. Eating together is a kind of bonding experience. Here, so close to the Middle East, eating has almost covenantal significance. When we eat together we become family. Your friends are my friends, your enemies are my enemies! I've got your back, you've got my back. In fact the common Turkish word for "friend" is *arkadaş*, the "one at your back." Living here it is easier to understand why the Jewish leaders were so upset with Jesus for eating with "tax collectors and sinners." See, for example Luke 5:30. You can almost hear the disgust in their voices. "He not only talks with them, he *eats* with them!" But in fact Jesus very deliberately chose to identify with them in this way. It was precisely for these people he had come.

It has long since become dark outside and now we would like to get home. It has been a long day and Betty is still not feeling 100%. I am tired and coming down with a cold. But there is no rushing away, besides we are having fun together. But after the usual false starts we head out. We hope to see them briefly once more, before we leave town on Sunday. I remind Jakub to read over the passage we had read earlier from the Bible. I tell him there will be a test on Sunday! Eventually we set off down the street, ten minutes walk to catch the bus.

Unfortunately we catch the wrong bus. It is going more or less to the right district, but with so many side trips we get totally turned around with no idea where we are. Eventually there is no one left on the bus but us. The and the driver asks where we are going. He doesn't know the street I mention. So I say we are looking for the last metro station, we know the way from there. Turns out it is not too far away and he graciously drives us over there. Would that ever happen back in Canada?

We walk the last part of our journey, weary, but glad for such a rich day. It is ten-ish when we get in the door, later than anticipated, but we are welcomed graciously. A quick check of email and off to bed.

Colossians 3:1-4   Radical Reorientation

Set your mind on things that are above, not on things that are on earth. For you have died, and your life is hidden in Christ in God.

....

O Lord, forgive me for being so enamoured with the toys of this world.

I am like a husband who keeps looking over his wife's shoulder at other women.

Jesus, I lift my eyes to you.

Help me to set my wandering mind on things above.

Thank you for Kaan, who lifts his eyes to you even while his head is down at shoe-level.

And Lord, rescue Jakub and his dear family from the runaway train.

I plead, in Jesus' name, Amen.

"Get out of our house! You are no child of ours!"

Turkish converts to Christ are not in danger of losing their lives, but they may lose their jobs, and their friends. And they may be disowned by their parents, who feel their son or daughter has betrayed them. How could they dishonour their family and community and religion in this way? They have abandoned all they have been brought up to value and hold dear. They might as well be dead!

And how close they are to the truth. We almost wonder if they have been reading Jesus: "If anyone comes to me and does not hate his own father and mother . . . and even his own life, he cannot be my disciple" (Luke 14:26); or Paul: "For you have died, and your life is hidden in Christ in God" (Col. 3:3).

For has not the new convert pledged allegiance to the flag of another kingdom? Has she not sold out to a new King? These Muslim parents may see more clearly than the average western church member the sweeping implications of signing up for Jesus. Our baptism is a funeral service first, and only then a celebration of life (Rom. 6:1-11).

Why do we Christians remain so attached to this world? Of course, we continue to live out our lives in God's creation, which is still good, despite the Fall. But this world, and the "prince of this world," are destined for destruction, like a run-away train headed for a washed-out bridge.

Praise God for his deliverance. In Christ he offers us eternal life! Yes, we who belong to Christ share in his death. But we also share in his *resurrection*. We share in his heaven-life. We share in his heavenly power and authority. We share in his future, public glory (Col. 3:4).

How wonderful when a whole family can experience this radical reorientation heavenward.

16. Language Drills

This morning I am the one feeling a little off, but Betty is much better. We leave the house about 9:30 to walk over to the metro for the ride down town. We are going to visit Selim again, this time in his work place. We expect Hamit to be there also. He is a retired math teacher, and was my language teacher when we lived here. I spent a lot of time with these two characters, going over verb forms, trying to participate in their animated discussions, and talking over and reading aloud the Scriptures. Reading aloud is a great way to learn a language. And it doesn't hurt if the text is familiar.

Hamit is also a believer. But his family are devout Muslims and life is difficult for him at home. They live literally up against the wall of a mosque in another district of the city. I was there once for a meal. Hamit has five children. One, still living at home, teaches at the local Çurkurova university (40,000 students). Some of his other children are grade school teachers. The youngest has epilepsy. It is good to see him again. We talk about our families, our current situation, our journey.

Under the coffee table in the waiting room I spot the backgammon board (*tavla* in Turkish). I've seen Selim and Hamit get into some high-pitched battles over that game. On a side table two love birds sit very close. It is a tender scene in a tough industrial building, on a tough street, in a tough part of town. Selim proudly shows me his new (to him) dentist equipment. He has been upgrading.

Why does he have so few customers? Perhaps because everyone on the street knows he belongs to a very small Christian minority. He once told me how he had been rounded up and arrested (along with tens of thousands) in the military coup of 1980. There in the miserable conditions of his jail cell Jesus came to visit him! He has been a different man ever since. He went in, a nominal Assyrian-background Christian; he came out, a devout follower of our Lord.

Selim makes tea for Betty and I and coffee for Hamit. Listening to the difficult life-stories of these men I attempt to encourage them by reading Ephesians 3:14-21. Here are the closing verses:

> . . . Tanrı, bizde etkin olan kudretiyle, dilediğimiz ya da düş-ündüğümüz her şeyden çok daha fazlasını yapabilecek güçtedir. Kilisede ve Mesih İsa'da bütün kuşaklar boyunca sonsuzlara dek O'na yücelik olsun! Amin.

> . . . Now to him who is able to do far more abundantly than all that we ask or think, according to the power at work within us, to him be glory in the church and in Christ Jesus throughout all generations, forever and ever. Amen.

These are stirring words in any language and I hear the murmurs of agreement from these two men. Selim says we should pray before we leave. I regret that my prayer is mostly in English. But the Spirit bears testimony to our unity in Christ.

Then it's time to go. It has been a long enough visit, especially for Betty who is a bit left out in this male environment. We carefully descend the poorly lit stairs and exit onto the street, blinking in the bright sunlight. Again we pass the guy with his hand cart who had called out to me two days earlier—another warm greeting. Then past Zafer in his little convenience store where I used to pick up water and one-cup packages of instant coffee on my way to Selim and Hamit for language class. He wants us to stay and talk, but we need to move on. Somehow I forget to put my head in to the little barber's shop whose son we found in Toronto. When we remember, it is too late to turn back.

We slowly pick our way through the hot, crowded, rabbit-warren streets of old Adana, trying not to get run over by cars and minibuses. The sidewalks are often blocked with parked vehicles. But eventually we reach our target, in a more upscale area of town. This is one of the few Christian book shops in the whole of the country. It is heavily subsidised, of course. It is hard enough for Christian bookstores to make a go of it even in so-called Christian Canada. We enjoy the coolness of the shop after the heat of the street, and take advantage of the nice, clean washroom. Davut, the gracious manager, makes tea for us.

We talk, though I find it especially hard to follow his accented Turkish, and I am not the only one. This man has faithfully served here for many years, often witnessing to curious passers-by, or to those who come in to use the photocopier. Just to have a Christian bookstore on a busy street, month after month, year after year, is a tremendous testimony in this challenging environment.

I stock up on some Turkish literature to pass out during the rest of the trip. Some will come back to Canada. It is not expensive, but there is a limit to what we can carry. The church is so young here that the body of Christian literature written by Turks is small. Most of the Christian books are still Turkish translations of English books. Josh McDowell's classic, *More than a Carpenter*, has been well received. I get a copy of Bruce Milne's book, *Know the Truth*, also a classic, and now in Turkish. And, of course, we stock up on Bibles and New Testaments. As we head out on to the Muslim street I am very conscious of the name of the Christian book store blazoned in large letters on the plastic shopping bag!

One more stop before we head back to home base. A couple of blocks away, on the ground floor of one of the modern apartment buildings that line the streets of this area of town, is our new friend, Mahir. How did we get to know this man and his family?

Well, when we lived in Toronto our church hired a cleaning company to come in a couple of times a week. Imagine my surprise when the couple who came turned out to be Turkish! Imagine their surprise when I spoke to them in their mother tongue! Over the next few years we had numerous impromptu discussion, reminiscences, Turkish lessons, debates about Turkish politics, etc. I also read to them from my Turkish Bible. They have an Alevi Muslim background.

One day, about three years ago, I mentioned that Betty and I were making a short trip back to Turkey. "Which part?" they asked. "Mostly Istanbul and Adana," I replied. "My brother lives in Adana!" she exclaimed. "Could you take a gift to him?" And so we met Mahir and his wife and two young boys.

Today we decide not to stay long. Mahir is usually not far from home since he is the custodian for that building. But his wife is out working, and the children are in school. We talk about family and our move away from Toronto to BC. He wants to make tea for us, but we have just had some. In spite of the brevity of the visit we still feel it is important. Very likely we are the first Christians ever to have been in his home. This is now my third visit. When will he encounter any other followers of Jesus? Remember our friend Mahir, O Lord.

Back out in the wilting heat (and this is October!) we walk over to catch the bus. On the way we stop to buy some fruit. The bus is sweltering and slow, but eventually we make it to our hop-off point, we got on the right bus this time. After purchasing one more large bottle of water we make our slow way down the streets to our home away from home. On arrival we discover the power is off, why and for how long, no one knows. This is how it is here. But there is still water in the taps and the roof-top solar water heater has been busy. The lukewarm shower is refreshing. We rest for a while and feel much better. Then the power comes back on and we send some emails. I spend an hour or so typing up notes. It's time to call it a day.

Colossians 3:5-11   Off With the Old

Put to death therefore what is earthly in you . . . put them all away . . . seeing that you have put off the old self with its practices and have put on the new self . . .

....

Heavenly Father, forgive me my sins (as I forgive those who sin against me).

Yet even more than this, help me to put away what remains of the earthly in me.

"Search me, O God, and know my heart! Try me and know my thoughts! And see if there be any grievous way in me, and lead me in the way everlasting!"
(Ps. 139:23-24)

For you, in your grace and mercy, have called me into a new life modeled after your own pure heart.

Help me Lord! Amen.

Once we attended a baptism service along the Mediterranean shore. It was a public place and some of us wondered how our Muslim neighbours would react. A passing couple asked what was going on. They sensed it was some kind of religious ritual. What a great opportunity to share the Gospel.

Baptism by immersion is such a marvelous picture of Christian conversion. The downward movement into the water is a kind of death. It would be death if the one being baptized was held under too long! But then comes the upward movement—with a splash and a gasp for air . . . resurrection! new life! new creation!

But what is portrayed so dramatically as *event*, is worked out in real time as *process*. The earthly elements within us linger on. We do not become instantly holy. Sanctification is a life-long process. Our earthly passions and desires still pull us toward impurity. Our mouths also need serious retraining. Paul spells out the ugly, unholy details (5, 8). And, inspired by the *Holy* Spirit of God, he calls us to deal with ungodliness seriously and severely—*put them all away! . . . put off the old self! . . .* even: *put to death! . . .* (*mortify* them, as the KJV put it).

What? Have we not already shared in the death and resurrection of Christ? Yes, but it appears we are called to an ongoing and deliberate engagement with his death, as well as with his resurrection.

These sins will not just walk away on their own. With God's help we must push back, we must give them no room. We will refuse to nourish them in any way. We will throw out inappropriate books, we will cancel the cable and cut the internet, if that's what it takes.

The world will scoff, but it is time to get as serious with sin as Christ was on that solemn cross.

17. Oranges Off the Tree

I have been coming down with a cold. Yesterday my nose ran, today a bit of a cough and a hoarse throat. We are staying inside at least for this morning and I will get a little bed rest. Fortified with extra vitamin C and garlic capsules (odourless!) I am feeling a little better. We want to visit Yusuf and Olgun today, an elderly couple we got quite close to when we lived here. Thankfully their home is just a short walk away.

Over the last few days there have been serious street riots across Turkey. Over twenty people have died, including police. People are trying to push the government into sending the army across the border to fight for the town of Kobane against the advance of ISIS. The government is willing to be part of a multi-national force but is reluctant to go in alone (a wise stance I believe). Meanwhile people are watching from this side of the border as their families and relatives struggle against the invasion of that city. I did pass one small protest group on the street a couple of days ago. It was pretty tame, and there were plenty of police present. But elsewhere in Adana there have been larger riots and one death. We did hear gunshots one night.

But overall it is peaceful here. Just the usual hustle and bustle of a busy Turkish city. Because of the unrest the trains between Adana and Mersin (passing Tarsus) were cancelled a couple of days ago. We wonder about our train to Ankara on Sunday evening. But as far as we know all trains are up and running again for now. If necessary we can leave earlier, perhaps by bus, and head further west, away from the hotspots, but so far we feel safe enough and the situation seems to be normalizing.

Two-o-clock rolls around and we walk over to see Yusuf and Olgun. Another warm welcome! When we lived here I spent an hour or so every Saturday with Yusuf. This continued for most of a year and Betty often came with me. Betty also took Turkish lessons from their daughter. We notice they look older and health problems accumulate. They have both had close calls with death. Fortunately their son and his wife live close by to keep an eye on them. They come over while we visiting. The daughter and her new husband also live nearby, but are away at the moment. As we drink tea Betty shows them our most recent family photos. There is lots of excited talking, some of which we even understand.

Though the rest of him is falling apart, Yusuf's mind remains bright. He has the heart of a teacher and is knowledgeable and interested in many things. I want to give him a Christian book but his eyesight is not so good now. We pray that our past talks and our warm friendship will pull him towards Jesus. Olgun is already a Christian, but not so active these days. In the past she has often attended church and Bible classes. Yusuf has been tolerant of her going, but resistant himself—a Muslim agnostic?

As we get up to leave, Yusuf takes us to one of the orange trees in his little garden and picks a couple of ripe oranges for us. Fruit straight from the tree, how nice is that? "Kendinize iyi bakın (Take care of yourselves)," we tell them. One last hug and cheek kisses for me from Yusuf. Will we see them again?—we hope so.

Now for some more exercise. Fifteen minutes walk takes us to the to the metro station. We have decided to become tourists for the rest of the day. We will ride the metro from end to end. Except for the underground sections we get a great view of the city, and the river, since we are crossing to the other side. The complete journey takes only 25 minutes—try doing that on the bus!

Another short walk and we are in the newest shopping mall in Adana. It's posh, expensive, and expansive, spread out over four floors. We put our bag through the metal detector and pass into the cathedral-like space. Here is the temple to universal god of materialism—the shopping mall—though we are disinclined to worship. We are only window shopping.

Up on the third floor food section we get a *kumpir*, a large roasted potato, with cheese melted into the inside. It is large enough for two of us and all the supper we need, with our usual *ayran* and water. The simple meal is much more expensive than it would be on the street, but we enjoy it. We also enjoy the air-conditioning and clean toilets. We sit and watch people pass by for a while. We seem underdressed for such a posh environment. This is so different from the street life we enjoy. In this mall we could be in any modern city anywhere.

Wandering around we notice a lot of English in the store names and advertising, something we rarely see on the street. And look!—there is even a small ice rink—in the "oven-city" of Adana yet! A middle-aged man is cautiously shuffling across the ice, perhaps his very first time on skates. Some teenagers are skating fairly confidently. But I don't think ice hockey will overtake football (soccer) here any time soon. One more trip to the upscale loos and we head out into the darkness to find the metro station again. For some reason the street lights are not working and we are glad of the car headlights.

At the station I tap the turnstile with my transit card to pay the two lira for Betty to get in. We like the hi-tech payment systems on public transportation in Turkey. But then I realize the security guard is pointing me over to another turnstile for me to pass through. It takes me a few seconds to realize why. Oops! I hadn't noticed that some turnstiles are for students only. They tick off a reduced rate from the transit card. Sometimes you save a few cents by not knowing what is going on (though mostly it is the opposite!) Next time I will be more careful.

As we get on the train there is a long announcement that we can't catch. But soon the train is moving. Since we are at the end of the line it has to be in the right direction. But we notice the train doesn't stop at one station, one we had previously used a couple of times when visiting friends. Perhaps that is what the announcement was about. Eventually we get to the far end of the line again, where we had begun earlier in the day. We make our way across the still busy streets to our home way from home. Along the way we pick up another large bottle of water. This is part of life in Turkey. We normally don't drink tap water, and we don't want to consume all the water of our generous hosts. Next day we learn that particular station had been closed because of riots in the area. The police were limiting the movement of people in and out of the district by closing off the station.

Colossians 3:12-14 — From Rags To Righteousness!

**Put on then,
as God's chosen ones,
holy and beloved,
compassionate hearts,
kindness, humility,
meekness... patience...
forgiving each other...**

....

*Heavenly Father,
is this holiness?*

*I was expecting horsehair
shirts and bare feet.*

*Your righteousness is
so beautiful...the colours!*

*For this you have chosen
me—to be called holy,
and to become holy.*

*And yet to love the
unlovely, that is so hard.
And to set aside my place
for the sake of others...
And to forgive, when I
have truly been wronged?*

*Help me Father.
Drench me Holy Spirit.
Abide in me Lord Jesus.*

*Will I really be like you
on that day?* (1 John 3:2)

*What gift... What grace.
Thank you Lord*

We hate to part with old clothes—"but those paint-covered slippers are so comfortable... those frayed jeans fit so well...!" Under cover of darkness we secretly recover our treasures from the garbage.

But in matters of the heart we are called to be ruthless. "Off with the old," says Paul. But then, gloriously, joyfully, tenderly, "On with the new!" And there, laid out on the bed, as it were, our Heavenly Father has new clothing ready for us.

Can these be mine?! Compassion? Kindness? Humility even? (Wait till my wife hears about this!) Meekness, Patience, a Forgiving heart?

How strange these clothes feel. They smell different. They are so clean... so white. They feel like Someone Else's clothes. And they are. We are clothed in His righteousness.

"Oh, I couldn't... It's not me... I would feel like a fraud." But no, I must put on this clothing. It is a gift of great price. Not to wear these things would be to dishonour the Giver. And so my joy overrides my shame. Grinning, I venture out on to the street where my neighbour looks twice and splutters to his wife, "Can a leopard change its spots?"

Well this one can, or rather the Spirit of God can! For is this not the New Covenant reality?—a new living heart replacing my old stony model, the Spirit empowering me to be good (Ezekiel 36:26-27).

But this is not just about "letting go and letting God." The text urges us to be fully engaged in the process. How carefully we dress ourselves each morning. After all, our clothes will not hang themselves on our body. The least we can do is put on what has been put out. And over all this, *put on love* (3:14), the ultimate fashion statement!

From rags to righteousness—what a gift! what a responsibility! what joy! what delight!

18. No Men Allowed

We won't do much exploring today because of the unrest in some areas of the city. Our host receives regular updates from the US consulate as to where the hot spots are. Betty decides to stay home to rest and pack for tomorrow's departure. I go out to get a haircut. My friend recommends a nearby place and the price I can expect to pay.

It is not hard to find. For one thing the towels hanging up outside to dry in the sun are the sure give-away of a Turkish barbershop. As I enter I am promptly given tea. That's kind of them. Then I see that everyone is drinking tea. I wonder which is the barber and how long I will need to wait. This is a typical cross-cultural experience. I don't know how to read the signs. I am not even sure what the signs are. But I can wait too. It will come clear. Suddenly two of the waiting men get up and leave. Had they just dropped in for tea? One man stays seated and the remaining chap turns back into a barber and resumes his work. Soon enough it is my turn. I don't get the same deal as my friend, but I won't complain. I get in some more Turkish practice and a good trim also.

Before returning home I walk out to the bus stop and head partway towards downtown, getting off at the second canal. There are quiet places to sit here overlooking the end-of-season modest flow of irrigation water. It is always a little cooler by the canal, it has its own micro-climate. For lunch I pick up a *simit* and a bottle of *ayran* to consume while I work on a newspaper. With the help of a dictionary I decipher a few paragraphs. Newspaper Turkish is hard. At least I get the sudoku right. On the way home I pick up some fresh, local fruit as a gift for our friends at our next port of call—the Black Sea coast. Orange trees won't grow in their back yard.

I get back home just in time to escape the rain. There I learn that the lady of the house has women coming in for a Bible lesson. My friend and I must leave—no men allowed! Besides, he has some shopping to do. Betty decides to join us. We get in his car and head off for the mall.

During our three years here I only drove once. It was enough. Turkish street culture is very different from Canadian street culture. (Not to mention the specialized language!) But there were other reasons we chose not to drive back then. You meet more people when you travel on public transportation. Nevertheless, when a rare rain does come to Adana, it is nice to be in a car, and our friend has been driving here for so long he has fully adjusted to the local street scene.

Before heading back home he takes us on a short detour alongside the scenic lake that backs up behind the dam across the Seyhan river. There are some fine homes up here, making the most of the water views. The air is cleaner and cooler too, compared to the crowded, low-lying downtown. Palm trees of various kinds, ornamental orange trees (with showy but inedible fruit) and semi-tropical flowering shrubs line the streets and boulevards. Turks have an eye for beauty. We appreciate our little tour. It is a gift after tramping across sometimes claustrophobic streets in search of our stray friends.

Colossians 3:15-17

Let the peace of Christ rule . . . Let the word of Christ dwell . . . singing . . . with thankfulness in your hearts to God.

. . . .

Thank you Father for adopting me into your family.

How precious, how vital, this has been to me.

Not only for my growth and maturity, but also, I think, for my survival.

Tea and prayers around the kitchen table, Thursday choir practice, coat-rack conversations, Turkish house-churches, bread and cup—together.

Your family, O Lord, makes me feel almost whole, almost normal.

To love and be loved, to know and be known, to serve and be served, how blessed I am!

With your people, O Lord, I hear your word better, I can worship again, I am thankful. Amen, I am thankful.

He Sets the Solitary In Families (Ps. 68:6)

"Off with the old; on with the new!"—the clothing metaphor works well as a description of the radical character transformation of the followers of Jesus.

But like all metaphors it has its limitations. And it is limited in this way: Paul is not writing to an individual, he is writing to the church. All the verbs and pronouns are plural.

So are we to be unclothed and re-clothed in public?! Not exactly—but the context of our spiritual transformation is life together in the family of God. How we independent westerners need this constant emphasis on God's new community, the church. The apostle presses this point home:

Loving relationships: *And let the peace of Christ rule in your hearts, to which indeed you were called in one body* (15). Kindness, humility, patience, forgiveness, and so on, are not academic exercises, but relational realities. Is it possible to enjoy peace in the church? By the grace of God, it is! The very peace (*shalom*) of Jesus is let loose among us.

Corporate reading: *Let the word of Christ dwell in you richly, teaching and admonishing one another in all wisdom* (16a). Let us be hospitable to the word of Christ, not assigning it to the cupboard under the stairs, or (worse) the woodshed, but welcoming the beloved word into every corner of our life together—"for teaching, for reproof, for correction, and for training in righteousness" (2 Tim. 3:16).

Harmonious worship: *singing psalms and hymns and spiritual songs, with thankfulness in your hearts to God* (16b). Are there days when I don't feel like singing?—of course there are! But as we worship together my reluctant heart is carried along on the song of my brothers and sisters. And I am swept up in thankfulness to God the Father. I praise you Lord for calling me into this dear "boot camp."

19. The Turkish face of Jesus

Sunday has arrive fast enough—our last day in Adana. Our breakfast is built around a boiled egg. For Betty and I this feels familiar. Back home my "preaching breakfast" consists of one boiled egg, one piece of toast without butter, and a cup of tea without milk. (My voice is clearer if I skip the dairy products.)

Unfortunately the lady of the house is not well today and will stay home and try to shake off this bug. But Betty and I jump in the car and go with our friend to his home church. This was our home church also when we lived here. We felt it was important to become committed members of a local congregation, even though we were foreigners and might not spend a long time here. How will the young Turkish believers learn the importance of belonging to the local church if we outsiders do not model it? Besides, we needed to belong also.

There are now four or five small groups of Christians gathering for worship in this city of three million souls. It may not sound like many, but fifteen years ago there were very few Christians here. It seemed impossible to establish a stable congregation and foreign workers would last only a short time. But then, at the beginning of the new millennium, there was a break through. Independently of each other (though not of God!) a solid group of mature workers moved in and stayed. Since then the church has put down good roots.

Back when we lived here, we and others encouraged our congregation to purchase a building. Renting is an ongoing hassle. The ever-present question-mark over where the church will be meeting next year is unsettling to these already fragile believers. Slowly funds began to accumulate. Then, soon after we moved away, with support from overseas, they were able to purchase this small apartment building. One floor has been opened up as much as the structure will allow. This is where the church meets for worship. Other rooms are used for Sunday school classes and other smaller meetings. Owning their own building also allows the church to be more firmly rooted in this particular neighbourhood. They work hard at getting to know their neighbours, helping them to see they do not need to be afraid of these strange Christians.

On our way in we stop to greet the three policemen stationed comfortably at an outside table. They are here for our security, being assigned to this task by the city. Harassment of churches is rare in Adana, but it has happened, and the city fathers don't want that kind of negative publicity. We sometimes wonder if the police come primarily for the coffee and cookies provided for them. They are a friendly presence. I understand the daughters of one of the officers are now actively involved in the church.

As we go inside we are warmly greeted by old friends and catch up on their news. How good it is to see these Turkish believers pressing on in the faith despite the challenging environment. One or two faces are missing, but there are many new faces also. The worship space is packed with 70 or 80 people. It seems to us there are still more foreigners than Turks (this is intended to be an international congregation) but the service is conducted in Turkish. Occasionally simultaneous English translation is provided through a headset system, but not today. If foreigners are going to live and work here they might as well get on with learning the language.

Some of the songs we know from our Canadian churches, or at least we know the melody and read the Turkish translation off the overhead screen. But the Turkish church has developed an impressive repertoire of its own home-grown hymns and songs. They have many gifted writers and composers. In their songs we seem to come closer to the Turkish face of Jesus. We find this deeply moving.

This service follows the outline of a typical service back home. Why would it not?—the church has been planted by folks from back home. I sometimes wonder what the church here will look like as it matures into a fuller Turkish identity. The young foreign worker preaches from 1 Corinthians 5, a tough passage in any language. But he handles it well and the crowd is attentive. Then it is upstairs for more fellowship over tea and coffee.

But we are not done with worship yet. After more drawn-out farewells we get back in the car for our next worship service. Today our host is the visiting preacher. This congregation has very few foreigners. Here we are getting closer to a truly Turkish worship service. It is noisy, happy, and participatory. Many different people take part in leading, announcing, reading scripture and praying. We love the way Turkish women feel free to pray openly during the prayer time. What a contrast with the men-only mosque activities, the women, if present, silently sectioned off behind a screen.

We are glad to see how this congregation is growing. There are many new young people in the crowd. Even in a mission frontier like Turkey it doesn't take long to settle into maintenance mode. But not this group. This is a mission-minded congregation. Their latest project is to start a new outreach in fresh territory on the eastern side of the Seyhan river.

Our friend preaches well. He'll never be mistaken for a Turk, but he has lived here for a long time and knows and loves these people. And he is proficient in the language. He is clearly connecting with the congregation.

In a separate space the church has set up a little café. Profits are going towards a building fund. They also long for a place to call their own. But with few relatively wealthy foreigners among the membership it will take a while for this group to raise enough money. On the other hand, when they are able to get settled in their own space, they will own it more deeply.

As I sip on my tea Kaan comes over and hands me back my old shoes, now thoroughly renovated, if not resurrected. Besides some stitching repairs he has re-soled them, something I was told couldn't be done back in Canada. I try to pay him but he refuses to take anything. He is pleased to do this for me. I try to figure out the Turkish for: "How beautiful are the shoes of those who bring Good News!" He laughs and finishes the sentence for me. Lord, remember your faithful cobbler and his lovely wife.

We are pleased to see a number of familiar faces here. Each has a remarkable story to tell. First generation conversions are often dramatic, especially in a Muslim setting.

This is also the home church of Selim and Birsen and their family. More hugs and kisses as we say goodbye to them too. How can we leave them?

How fragile the little churches appear in this large, modern, Muslim city. But how lovingly they are watched over by the Shepherd. How carefully he tends each member of his flock. And is he not also the King of kings, having more authority and power than all the earth's empires rolled into one? If He is for them, who can stand against them?

How insignificant these little groups appear to the uninitiated. Big money and big media are not even aware they exist. But how different this world appears when viewed from above. In truth these humble churches are outposts of life and light in a confused and lost world. When the time of shaking comes it will be obvious to all that they are founded on the Rock. And what seemed weighty has disappeared like chaff in the wind.

Now at last we have time for a mid-afternoon meal. We want to take our generous hosts out for a nice meal before our departure. Unfortunately our friend's wife is still not able to join us. When we ask him to recommend a place he suggests a restaurant run by a family he has come to respect highly. These good Muslims are concerned for the homeless people in Adana. They take in two or three at a time and teach them to wash dishes and wait on tables, and so become employable. Our friend likes to support this family enterprise and we are happy to join him. We sit outside under the warm sun and enjoy the good food. What a life!

When we left this morning we threw our suitcases into the trunk of the car. Now our friend graciously drives us around to the train station and bids us farewell. This is not the first time these faithful workers have taken us under their wing. We appreciate the gift of their hospitality. They are tuned in to the welcoming heart of our Heavenly Father. We look forward to seeing them again, hereafter, if not here.

Standing in front of the old train station, we admire once again, the stately building and its backdrop of tall palms. The first trains arrived in Adana in 1886, but the initial building was too small for a rail system that would soon link Europe to Baghdad. The present, very fine building was completed in 1912.

It is pleasantly cool inside. We find the right platform and a convenient bench. Trains come and go frequently, and passengers pass by in waves, but our overnighter will not leave until later in the evening. I make sure Betty is comfortable and leave her with the luggage while I run over for a last, brief visit with Jakub. I promise to be back in an hour.

It has been so good to see Jakub again. "I wish you would move back onto my street," he says. I would like that too, but there are other addresses laying claim to our lives. I notice the Bible is not in its plastic bag, he has been reading it between customers. I remind to read from the marker we left in John's Gospel. I tell him I read from the Bible almost every day. If he does the same our spirits will be traveling in the same direction. He likes that. It is soon time to get back to Betty but he steps over to his tree and picks three oranges, taking care to choose the biggest. One last hug and I am off. I wonder if I will see him again. Please Lord.

As I tear down the street, suddenly there is our custodian from the old apartment building. He has bottles of *pekmez* with him. *Pekmez* is a kind of molasses made from grape juice. Every fall he spends a week back in his mountain village home. There they take the grape juice and boil it down, somewhat like the maple syrup process. He must have recently returned from such a "holiday." The fall we were living here he gave us a bottle. *Pekmez* is delicious. I especially like it with plain yoghurt. It seems very un-Turkish, but I have time only for the briefest of greetings before I dash back to the station.

Colossians 3:18-4:1

Whatever you do, work heartily, as for the Lord and not for men, knowing that from the Lord you will receive the inheritance as your reward.

....

Heavenly Father, thank you for speaking into my here/now life.

Today, this hour, here is the way of Jesus, and I may choose to walk in it.

Help me Lord to agape-love my wife letting it cost if need be.

May my leadership of my children & grandchildren be for their best good, not to dis- but en-courage.

In my work, deliver me from trying to "look busy" instead, from the heart, may I work for you, this whole day.

Deliver me Lord from my clamouring self-interest, for your glory (and my joy) Amen

Where the Rubber Meets the Road

The cynic quips: "Those Christians are so heavenly-minded they are no earthly good." But how wrong they are! It is precisely their heavenly-mindedness that makes Christians so down-to-earth. It is life "in the Lord" (18), "pleasing the Lord" (20), "fearing the Lord" (22), "for the Lord" (23), "from the Lord" (24), and "under the Lord" (4:1), that radically transforms the daily practicalities of marriage, family, and work.

Remarkably, and in deep contrast to the Jewish-Greek-Roman world, wives, children, and slaves are not overlooked here. In Christ their personhood is highlighted. In fact they are addressed *before* their husbands, fathers, and masters (respectively).

So is Paul preaching a "Liberation Theology"? —well, Yes and No. He is not preaching against order and hierarchy. If we are created in the image of our Triune God, in whom there is order and hierarchy, we will expect to see the same in our marriage and family life.

Neither is Paul advocating that slaves rebel and Christian masters dismiss their servants. That would lead to societal chaos, and homelessness and hardship for the slaves, at least initially. Though, as we sense in Paul's letter to Philemon, when slave and master become brothers in the Lord, the days of the slave-master arrangement are numbered.

Yet Paul is preaching a greater and more urgent liberation here—this is liberation from the tyranny of the self and self-interest.

Wives and husbands, children and parents, are to be concerned with the interests of the *other*. The servant is to see that the master is well served (even when he is not looking!) And the master is to see that his slave is treated fairly.

Into our gritty, earthly realities—*Freedom!*

20. North to the Black Sea

There is a dining car on the train, but it is expensive, and we are never quite comfortable leaving our belongings alone in our compartment. So we stock up on a few portable edibles, we won't want to eat much anyway after that large meal, and settle down to enjoy the hum of the station, and perhaps read a little as we wait.

Even though departure time is a couple of hours away our train is already in the station. But we see that the sleeping car, back at the tail end, is not even close to the platform. After a final tidy up the train will be pulled forward. Until then we will wait where we are. The patient conductor is already fending off enough over-anxious local travelers without a couple of foreigners bothering him.

The station is naturally busy and noisy. But as the departure time draws near the huge electrical generator that powers our train suddenly fires up alongside us and the decibels head skyward. Betty decides she can hold out a bit longer. I wander off up the platform to take a few photos of the sun setting over the tracks. I remember to ask the security guard for permission first! I don't want to get my knuckles rapped as I did for taking a photo at the metro station a couple of days earlier. Local commuter trains continue to come and go, east to Iskenderun, or west to Tarsus and Mersin.

Then, at last, an engine backs towards us and is attached to the front of our train. I guess I am just a little boy at heart revelling in the wonder of these great iron beasts. I peer down from the platform watching carefully to see that everything is hooked up properly. Satisfied with his work, the mechanic climbs out of the way and the train is moved forward for loading. As the *hoi poloi* scramble for a good seat in the forward cars, we saunter like seasoned travelers down to the far end where the conductor shows us to our reserved compartment.

We have taken overnight trains before in Turkey. It is still a very affordable way to travel here. As expected our little room has a small fridge (containing complementary snacks), a sink, towel, slippers, good lighting and air conditioning. With the two bunk beds folded up our compartment feels roomy. We relax in our spacious comfort and privacy.

For some time we sit with the lights out looking through the window. But with the sun down there is not much to see once we leave the city behind us. So we eat a little, read a little and I catch up with my notes. Then we ask the conductor to lower the bunk beds (it takes a special key) and we make it an early night. As we dose off, the train slowly makes its way up the Taurus mountains along the precipitous route we have come to know well.

Nearing the top, as the mountain face becomes too steep, we will pass through numerous tunnels with their fine, stone-arched openings. The building of this line (opened in 1918) was a major engineering feat. Then we will slip through the dramatic pass known in earlier times as the Cilician Gates (very familiar to the apostle Paul in his travels to the interior) before running slightly downhill to emerge from the foothills onto the Anatolian Plateau, the bread basket of the country. It could be Saskatchewan, with vast fields, and grain elevators every twenty minutes along the tracks.

We wake about 6:30 and wash and clean up for the day. Behind us the sunrise is spectacular. We are in the very last car, so I walk to the back and take some pictures of the disappearing rails glowing in the sun. The rolling prairies are behind us now and the terrain is more rugged. Off in the distance is a huge marble quarry. Marble is common here and inexpensive (only poor people have marble countertops!) The train was supposed to arrive in Ankara at 7:30, but we must have lost some time during the night. We are running an hour late. So we have lots of time to make a breakfast out of our remaining food. Racing across this beautiful countryside with the morning sun rising over us it seems a good day to start off with Psalm 19:
> *The heavens declare the glory of God,*
> *and the sky above proclaims his handiwork.*

We pray, then pack, then watch and wait.

And so we arrive in Ankara. As we climb down from the train, luggage bouncing behind us, we remember to leave a tip with the conductor. In planning this trip I discovered, on line, directions for getting from the train to the metro through an underground passage. The metro will then whisk us across town to the bus station. But this plan fails, as we run into a solid brick wall, literally. We discover the whole area is under major construction and, for now, there is no easy way to get to the metro. So on to plan B, which is to take a taxi, first crossing a major street so we catch a taxi going in the right direction (and save some fare.) Sixteen liras later we arrive at the huge *oto gar* known as *AŞTİ*, an acronym for Ankara Intercity Terminal Administration (the acronym works in Turkish!)

We have heard that, of the hundreds of buses leaving this terminal daily, three could take us directly to our destination on the Black Sea coast. We start asking and looking. The best we can do is a bus that leaves at noon. Perhaps if the train had come in on time we would have been able to leave earlier. But that is water under the bridge. Nothing for it but to wait. I purchase tickets for our numbered seats, the cashier noting that we are a couple. Single travelers are segregated according to gender.

AŞTİ is huge. As the hub of Turkey's intercity bus system it needs to be. Buses roar in and out on three levels. For the convenience of the traveling public there is direct, covered access to the metro. Betty and I take turns watching our luggage while the other wanders. The toilets (one lira per visit) are reasonably clean. There are plenty of places to buy snacks and drinks, but newspapers are scarce for some reason. We don't need to patronize the two restaurants we see. We want to save space for the large meal we are expecting later.

At one point I overhear a young woman talking to a security person. She is crying and upset. Sounds like someone has stolen her luggage. The guard doesn't sound very sympathetic. "You should watch over your belongings," he tells her. But perhaps there is compassion too, underneath his sternness. She does seem to have her purse with her.

I peer over a railing to look down on a lower level. There, far below, is a bus getting its huge windshield replaced. I wonder if a low-flying Canada goose was responsible. These are large modern coaches and replacing that won't be cheap. One guy uses a cordless, electric caulking gun to seal the new glass in place, casually tossing his empty cartridges onto the ground. It will be someone else's job to clean them up. The glass crew works very efficiently and soon the bus is as good as new. As I watch, a guy comes over to me starts up a conversation. Before long he asks me for a cigarette. When I tell him I don't smoke he loses interest and wanders off. It is a universal scenario.

Slowly the clock ticks towards high noon, our departure time. Since there are hundreds of intercity coaches coming and going we double check that we do have the right *peron*, platform. The *kapitan* will not wait around for lost passengers. So as our bus pulls in we are ready. I hand our luggage to the attendant who stores them in the underbelly of the beast and hands us in return a numbered stub. Will we see our luggage again? We always have in the past.

It turns out our seats are at the very back of the bus. This gives us a little more room to spread out. The sky is overcast now, but still dry. Thankfully it is cooler here than it was in Adana. The view from the window is ever absorbing and ever changing as we speed along a new, six-lane, divided highway. How does Turkey pay for all these new infrastructure projects?

As soon as we get out on the road the attendant comes down the aisle with refreshments. Strangely we do not get the customary splash of eau-de-cologne on outstretched hands. Has this quintessentially Turkish practice gone out of style? Or is it simply that the bottle is empty? We are offered coffee, tea, water and juice, plus a choice of something sweet to nibble on. On this bus each seat has its own video screen. But we don't have earphones and none are offered. We alternately doze and enjoy the scenery. For the first leg our journey the land is dry, with sandy hills on either side. It reminds us very much of our new hometown of Merritt, BC.

At one point we pass a large manufacturing facility with numerous buildings scattered over an extensive compound. We are surprised to see, at the center of the operation, a large, new-looking, two-minaret mosque. This is for the convenience of the workers, no doubt. Is this one of the "Anatolian Tigers," the new and prospering businesses springing up across the heartland of Turkey, highly supportive of the current, openly Islamic, ruling party?

As we head north the land levels out again and starts to look greener. We see farmers out doing their fall plowing. Occasionally we pass a lonely house, far from the nearest town. But this is very rare. Even in the open countryside most people live in villages under the shadow of the mosque.

As we get closer to the Black Sea coast we notice the steep roofs on the houses, a sure sign of a rainy climate. We have left the semi-desert of the interior plains behind. Here the countryside is green, green. Though there are still solar hot water heaters on the rooftops, so apparently they do still see the sun. The warm, damp climate here is perfect for the production of hazelnuts. Seventy-five percent of the world's hazelnut crop is grown in a 30km wide strip along almost the entire Turkish coast of the Black Sea. The easternmost end of this strip is taken up with tea production. Turkey's per-capita tea consumption is the highest in the world, and most of that tea is home-grown.

As we near the end of our journey the landscape is once again steep and rugged as we navigate the coastal mountains. From the highway we look down on lovely villages nestled in the valleys. From the chimneys we see smoke rising, and along the roadside there are long stacks of firewood. We have traveled a long way from sun-scorched Adana in the last 24 hours. We also notice something unusual for Turkey, fields with fences, and cattle or sheep sometimes without a shepherd. As we crest one more hill, suddenly there is the sea. One more leg of this pilgrimage is behind us. It's on to another adventure.

Colossians 4:2-6 Two Salty Conversations

Continue steadfastly in prayer, being watchful... making the best use of your time... Let your speech always be gracious... seasoned with salt... to answer each person.

....

Thank you Father, for you are neither dumb nor deaf.

Forgive me for my lazy, sleepy, repetitive, boring, tasteless prayers— how do you stay awake?

"May the words of my mouth and the meditation of my heart be acceptable [delightful, memorable] in your sight" (Ps. 19:14).

And out of the overflow of my thankful heart, may I be quick to speak of your grace, to the people you bring into my life.

May my savoury words draw them in to your heavenly feast table before their clock ticks no more. Amen.

We are created in the image of the God who speaks. So it is no surprise that we are talkers, some more than others! Now, in these four verses, Paul sketches out a practical theology of speaking.

And he focuses on two conversations, two speaking directions—the first upwards, God-wards, the second sideways, out-wards.

These conversations are to be ongoing and concurrent, at least potentially. Can you keep two conversations going at once? This is challenging for single-taskers like me.

Continue steadfastly in prayer, and perhaps, when not actually putting prayer into words, at least maintain an attitude of *watchfulness*, heavenly alertness. Prayer is a measure of how un-secular we are. Secular people don't pray, why would they? But we take the unseen world seriously.

Our talks with our Heavenly Father do not meander like kitten-tossed yarn, but are deliberate, purposeful, steadfast, wide-awake conversations seasoned with thanksgiving.

By the way (writes Paul) you might include us, the prisoners, in your prayers. Pray for an open door. Surprisingly, however, he is not referring to prison doors, but for an open door for the Word!

Do we have these same priorities? Paul leads us in this direction. Interact as wisely as possible with the not-yet-believers you meet in everyday life, *making the best use of the time.* He uses marketplace language—*ek* + *agora,* a 'shopping spree,' buying up all of a particular commodity.

Using every opportunity to speak with grace to each person. Who knows if we will meet again? But not sugar-coated words, please—salty words, tangy, unforgettable. We just can't do this from a distance. We need face to face, nose to nose, evangelism.

21. Chestnuts Roasting...

Why have we made this side-trip to the Black Sea coast?

Nine years earlier were looking for a place to call home in the sprawling metropolis of Istanbul. We had moved to Turkey to get to know Turks and to learn the Turkish language. Thus we chose to look for an apartment away from the international heart of the city where we would be tempted to speak English and hangout with other foreigners. In God's providential care we ended up in a suburb on the Asian side, about 20 minutes by commuter train from the Bosporus. There in that apartment building we met a family that has become very precious to us. The parents, Rasim and his wife Solmaz, were by then, retired. Rasim had been a school principal, Solmaz a teacher. As is the Turkish custom their unmarried son, Birkan, still lives in the family home. He is an engineer with the city. We cannot make a trip to Turkey without visiting this family.

Years ago, along with their extended family, they had purchased a three-unit apartment building in a small town along the Black Sea coast. This was to be their summer home during school vacation time. After the parents retired they spent half the year there, returning to their Istanbul apartment for the colder months only. Once, while we still lived beneath them in that Istanbul suburb, they invited us to spend a weekend at their summer place. It was a memorable time. And now, a decade later, we are returning for a second visit.

We scramble to get off the bus and collect our luggage before the driver takes off for the next port of call. Then, with the meagre battery time left on the phone, we call Birkan as arranged, and he comes to pick us up. How good it is to see his smiling face again. He is taking some holiday time to be with us during our stay. A short five minute drive from the *otogar* and we arrive at the familiar street.

What a warm greeting we receive as we get out of the car. Betty and Solmaz embrace and kiss like long-lost sisters. I get bristly cheek kisses from Rasim. They seem unchanged from our last meeting in Istanbul, three years ago. With typical Muslim modesty Solmaz wears a headscarf while I (an unrelated male) am here. But this does nothing to diminish the warmth of our friendship, or dampen the frequent laughter that fills the room. This is the family that first introduced us to the traditional face of Turkey. How civilized they are, how courteous and thoughtful. From them we have learned how to welcome strangers.

Solmaz and Rasim occupy the top floor of the building with a room permanently reserved for Birkan. One of the married sons has the middle floor. Since that apartment is unoccupied at the moment this will be our home for the one night we stay here. We are shown around and invited to rest awhile and enjoy some privacy. But we want to make the most of our short time here and are soon back upstairs. Over tea and special pastries made by Solmaz we catch up on the news. Betty exegetes her latest family photo, leaving a copy with

Solmaz who is very pleased. It seems only yesterday that we last saw them, except that some of the grandchildren in the photo were not born then.

Before dinner Birkan takes us out for a walk. First east along the beachfront. Too bad it is so late in the year. On our previous trip here we swam in the sea. The sand was almost too hot for our bare feet. The Black Sea takes its name from the black sand along the shore. (In Turkish, *Kara Deniz*—Black Sea; *Ak Deniz*—White Sea [Mediterranean]) Today it is overcast and nippy, but still a good day for a brisk walk. We enjoy the sound of the waves washing up along the beach. We pass a bride and groom having artsy wedding photos taken with an old rowing boat for a prop. She must be chilly in that dress! I snap a photo of my own and get a smile and a wave in return. On the horizon we see a few natural gas rigs perched on the water. These supply about 7% of Turkey's needs. But Turkey has, for the most part, missed out on its share of the great energy recourses of the Middle East. Though they may yet find something off the coast of Turkish Cyprus. The Black Sea is more famous for its fish than its oil, and we see many fishing boats gathering their catch as we saunter along hoping to find some treasure along the waterline.

In 1994 a wooden bust of Lenin, thought to have been dumped into the Black Sea during the fall of the Soviet Union in late 1980s, washed up on this beach. Since then there has been a heated and ongoing debate about whether to display the bust in a public park or not. Turkey historically has had no love for Lenin and his ilk and was a fiercely anti-communist ally of the US during the Cold War. Although the current left-leaning mayor of the town is in favour of the park option, the controversial beach bargain is still stored in the warehouse of the town council awaiting its fate.

Still empty-handed we turn and walk back westward towards the harbour, sheltered from the winter storms by a huge break water. We climb up onto the rock wall and walk out to the end. From here we can look back on the town. The low sun briefly breaks through the clouds over the water and I snap a couple of pics as fishing boats return to their safe haven.

We are not the only ones enjoying the late afternoon light. As we turn back an elderly man offers us a couple of cooked chestnuts. Taking our cue from Birkan we accept them and nibble away. Perhaps this man just wants to talk, this being his way of breaking the ice. We learn that he was the unexpected survivor of a terrible vehicle accident. He had been placed in the morgue already, along with other victims of the accident. But a Jewish doctor saw that he was still alive and worked to save him. The talk continues, of where he is from and his former work. Eventually we politely take our leave and turn for home. The world is full of lonely people just wanting to talk, even here in sociable Turkey.

When we see the special food Solmaz has prepared for us we are glad of our appetite-buttressing walk. What a spread it is! First comes a bowl homemade traditional soup, with lots of special local bread on the side. (Many regions of Turkey have their own distinctive bread.) There is a little dish of yogurt for each of us. Watching closely what the others are doing, we squeeze some lemon over our soup and add pepper. It is delicious. Then comes a dish of very tender meat balls, with slices of boiled potato in a rich broth. And lastly, homemade macaroni, a traditional Turkish recipe, with rice wrapped in grape leaves alongside. Solmaz harvested the grape leaves from their own garden earlier in the year, putting them in the freezer. We sprinkle some dry goat cheese over the macaroni. It is all very good. We politely refuse seconds. We are full—though not too full for tea and a sweet sesame desert.

All of this happens slowly, of course. This is not fast food. Besides we have much to talk about. Betty remembers the gifts she has brought and they have gifts for us also. I ask Rasim what he is writing these days. He is also an amateur author. He is glad I remember and disappears to get his most recent production, a book on his family roots going back to the 16th century. He signs a copy and gives it to me. He is already working on a second edition since more information has come in from other family members.

Then someone remembers the chestnuts they harvested nearby earlier in the fall and Birkan takes a bowlful and carefully cuts the side of each one before they are put in the oven. While the chestnuts are roasting the hazelnuts come out. They had an extra large harvest from their own hazelnut bushes this fall. We are given a generous bagful to take home. The hot chestnuts are just as delicious as we expect them to be. We sit back, full and content in many ways. How amazing that we should have such dear friends in a small town on the Black Sea coast, in far off Turkey. How good God is to us. It is time to disappear to the lower apartment and give thanks for all this before we fall asleep.

Colossians 4:7-18

Tychicus will tell you all about my activities . . . with him Onesimus . . . Aristarchus greets you and Mark . . . and Justus . . . Epaphras . . . Luke . . . Demas . . . Give my greetings to the brothers at Laodicea, and to Nympha and the church in her house.

....

Heavenly Father (so glad you are not just Heavenly Being, or Heavenly Force) . . . Heavenly Father, thank you for the blessed gift of friendship.

Teach me, Lord Jesus, to be the truest of friends, not in it for what I can get out of it, not even for conversions ('friendship' evangelism?) but for the love of your people, for whom you were willing to die.

Dear Holy Spirit, so drench me with your true fellowship, that my true fellowship with my neighbours will make them dream of you. Amen.

In the Image Of Our Relational God

And so Paul signs off with this long list of names and greetings. It is so personal—so relational. Yes, Paul can argue and debate with the best of them. He can soar to rhetorical heights in praise of his Lord. He can turn Gospel street-fighter, too, when his message is under attack. But beneath all that, is his love for his Lord, and his love for his Lord's people —toughness wrapped in tenderness. We sense how much Paul loved these folk, and how much they loved him.

Tychicus and Onesimus will hand-deliver this letter and fill the Colossians in on how things are with Paul in prison. And those with Paul in prison (fellow prisoners and helpers) are anxious to add their greetings to Paul's.

Notice how Paul looks for opportunities to affirm and encourage: *beloved brother . . . faithful minister . . . welcome him . . . faithful, hard-praying Epaphras . . . Luke the beloved physician . . . Nympha who hosts a church in her house . . . .*

Paul's Gospel is not about solitary conversions, it is about being welcomed into a Relational Kingdom, a New Community, the Body of Christ, the Family of God, where all are brothers and sisters *in Christ*. We are created in the image of our God who is one-in-three and three-in-one. We are created in the image of a relational God. Sin severs relationships. But God, in Christ, has made a way for us to be reconnected, to become truly human again.

In our friendships surely we come close to the heart of our Trinitarian God. And in our friendships with non-Christians we draw them in close also. We draw them into alignment with the very heart of God, a heart full of love and grace—we tug them heavenwards. Authentic friendships are redemptively subversive.

22. Fish and Cats

Breakfast is at 8:30. But we are up earlier, to read and pray, to shower and talk about our day. At the appointed time we venture upstairs to a warm reception. We remind our hosts that on our earlier visit, seven years ago, we had eaten on the balcony, shaded from the strong summer sun by a giant Coca-Cola umbrella. The balcony has since been upgraded with built in awnings of more sedate colours, but it is too cold now to eat out anyway. We are glad of the new natural-gas-fired heating system as we sit down to another generous Turkish breakfast, three different kinds of cheese, bread, honey, jam, boiled eggs, preserved figs, olives, and more. And tea, of course, without which the day shall not begin. Again, another slow meal, with lots of conversation, our heads spinning as we try to follow what is being said, or try to make a contribution. We are glad of Birkan's presence to help us out with a forgotten word, or simply to translate for us when we get stuck.

After a little rest and some packing, we all head off to the *pazaar* in Birkan's car. Tuesday is market day in this town and we can't miss this event. Obviously the whole population feels the same way and the streets are packed. People arrive on all methods of transportation imaginable, from little two-wheel tractors to large trucks, and everything in between. Parking is almost impossible.

Most of this *pazaar* is now under permanent roofing, open on the sides and ends but no need to put up tarps. But, of course, a *pazaar* will always extend beyond any attempt at boundaries, and we wander along a block or two of old-fashioned street market before we get to the massive covered area. What is for sale?—almost anything. Fruit and vegetables of all kinds, dried fruit and nuts, many different kinds of cheeses, clothes in all shapes and sizes, small household goods, pots and pans, textiles, bags, and small electronics. It is a riot of colour and bustle.

In one area the tables are very small, though also overflowing. Here village people come to sell from their own gardens. We see many kinds of mushrooms harvested from the woods and dried. Probably most of them are safe but we don't feel like experimenting. After looking around for a while I buy a pair of pants. Solmaz is buying her week's supply of fruit and veg. Betty gets some clothes for the grandchildren. We picked up a neighbour on the way here and she also gets her supplies. How will we reassemble our small group in this melee? But this is the age of cell phones. A quick call and we are soon together again. We squeeze into the car with our bundles and prizes and stories.

For lunch our friends want to take us to a fish restaurant. Because we are on the Black Sea coast this is the place for fish lovers, and we love fish. We opt to sit outside overlooking the entrance to the harbour. The weather is just warm enough, cool but no wind. Below us on the rocks cats gaze up at us and wait optimistically. We eat three different kinds of fish, nicely cooked with a very light batter. They are all small fish, the first reminds us of smelts, the last may be anchovies. What a treat.

Then it is time to head back to finish packing and leave for Istanbul with Birkan in his car. Our time here is so short, but very special. This family seems delighted with their strange Canadian friends. We each reach across our cultural and linguistic divide and meet more or less successfully in the middle, always with warmth and love. How we pray that they may come to know our Jesus. Then our joy will be complete. Father with you all things are possible. Will it not bring glory to your name, to bring these people safely home?

Birkan is a good driver. We wind our way up over the coastal mountain range and down into Duzce, stopping at the halfway point of our journey for a bathroom break and a leg stretch. In Duzce we join the toll highway, but it is very inexpensive. Birkan holds the transponder up to the windshield as we pass through the gate and it beeps a welcome. This region was severely damaged in the 1999 earthquake that claimed 45,000 lives. We drive through large areas of newly constructed apartment towers and extensive industrial areas. This part of the world has always been earthquake prone. We see the evidence in the ancient cities as well as in more recent times. People rebuild and move on as they have for millennia. Istanbul, a city of more than 15 million, sits on its own fault line and is at high risk for a major earthquake. Turkey is constantly working to upgrade buildings and building codes to reduce the potential for damage.

As we enter the Eastern suburbs of Istanbul we pull off the toll road and navigate the local streets to get to our next home base, the neighbourhood where we once lived for a year and a half, and home of these good friends. Our old building looks very different. In the past year the exterior received a layer of insulation covered with stucco and paint. Balcony railings were also upgraded. Birkan chaired the meetings of the apartment owners as they planned for these upgrades. Not everyone was onside but it was a good move and looks very sharp.

We might have walked right past, not recognizing the new face of the building. But the inside is familiar and we feel very much at home. These older Turkish apartments are spacious with lots of windows and light. Birkan prepares some soup and bulgur for us. He is a good cook. He has to be unless he wants to eat out a lot. For half the year he lives here alone. Now he is glad to have our company and we are well cared for. It turns out we will sleep in the bed of Solmaz and Rasim. Who would have imagined that, nine years ago! As we lie on their bed we pray for them. May the Lord grant them a life transforming dream of Jesus, as he has done for so many Muslims.

Philemon 1-3

To Philemon our beloved fellow worker and Apphia our sister and Archippus our fellow soldier, and the church in your house.

....

Heavenly Father, forgive me for my love of privacy and independence.

How easily I walk away, not just from people, but from your people, my family.

These inner trials and struggles, hidden behind my privacy fence—are they truly in need of such careful protection?

O Lord, you have promised that all will one day be proclaimed from the rooftop (Lk 12:3).

Crack open my shell, O Lord, and bind me more deeply and honestly to my brothers and sisters.

Perhaps I can learn here from my more openhearted Turkish family. Amen.

Philemon's Laundry—For All To See!

Twelve letters, Paul wrote . . . plus one. Twelve great letters, full of teaching and instruction for the church, plus this one personal letter to Philemon—coming to us almost like an afterthought, the extra bun thrown into the basket for good measure—a baker's dozen. And we wonder "why?"

Why, when the Bible is so economical with words, do get this little letter thrown in, so personal and intimate? (Wouldn't you rather know how Jesus explained the old prophecies to the disciples on the road to Emmaus?—for example.) Is Paul's private appeal to Philemon to receive back his runaway slave Onesimus Scripture-worthy?

It is, apparently: it is to the Holy Spirit, and it is to the church which down through the ages has so treasured this letter.

In this little gem we see one of the great themes of the Christian message. Who is worth less than a slave, in Roman society? And who is worth less than a runaway slave? But in the upside-down Kingdom of God, Onesimus is loved, and named, and memorialized alongside the great Apostle Paul. Jesus loves the little people too!

Then again, in this letter we see the final answer to slavery. Paul does not attempt to rid society of slavery through revolution, or violence. He simply preaches Christ to both master and servant. And when each receive Him they find themselves brothers in the One Family—how cool is that?!

In fact this letter never was written as a private letter to Philemon. It was written also to Apphia, Archippus, and "the church in your house." Because how the Philemons of this world respond to the Onesimus's of this world is simply not a private matter. Philemon will best learn the Christian way, not in private, but in community.

23. Historic Faith

After breakfast together (Birkan has a late start to his workday today) we leave my latest pants at the neighbourhood tailor to be shortened then walk over to the new underground metro that now passes through here. This is part of 30kms of underground metro completed in the last couple of years. Birkan has lent us his "Istanbul Kart" (electronic ticket) which we load up with 20 liras at the machine then click ourselves through the turnstile. What a great metro extension this is, so clean and nicely decorated. Through the day trains run every five minutes, then every three minutes in rush hour. Even so, at late morning, it is busy and we stand most of the way.

We jump off at the exchange station where we can catch the Marmary subway that crosses beneath the Bosporus. In fact we much prefer to cross on the ferries, but we would like to say that we have been through the Bosporus tunnel once, at least. Nine years earlier we discovered there were Japanese women sitting alongside us in our Turkish language classes. Japanese women learning Turkish? Turned out these women were the wives of the engineers partnering with Turkey on the building of the historic underwater tunnel. On our many ferry crossings we were able to observe the construction process as engineers using boat-mounted cranes prepared the floor of the Bosporus for the pre-cast tunnel sections. Now the project is complete.

We stay on this subway as far as Yenikapi. It was here that the entire Marmaray project was put on hold for four years as excavations revealed the remains of a long lost harbour dating back to pre-Roman times. Over the centuries it had gradually silted in to the point where the city simply expanded onto the new land and new harbours were built further out. This site turned out to be an archaeological treasure trove with many ancient boats recovered almost intact, along with their equally ancient cargo. Eventually the archaeologists gave the thumbs up and subway construction could continue. Under the high domed ceiling at the Yenikapi station there are displays illustrating the results of the dig, but most of the artifacts have been moved to Istanbul University and to nearby museums until the new Yenikapi museum is complete.

From the station we work our way back eastward, on foot, towards the historic peninsula and with its famous 500-year-old Sultanahment (Blue) Mosque and the glorious 1500-year-old Hagia Sophia Church building, now a museum. It's a good twenty-minute walk through some narrow and dodgy streets. We would not have come this way if we had not wanted to see the Yenikapi station. I'm glad I have Betty with me to keep me safe! But we run into no trouble and eventually the streets widen and the buildings become more substantial. We've just explored a new part of Istanbul.

Then, suddenly, the famous landmarks appear between the rooftops, soaring high and dominating the streetscape. This famous area is familiar to us from numerous visits. We won't take the time or spend the money to go inside, but we do enjoy these historic buildings. We look around to see what new restoration work has been done since we were last here.

Leaving the busy street behind us we pass under a stone archway set in a high wall and wander through the grounds of the old Ottoman (Topkapı) palace, for four centuries home to the sultans of the empire. We discover a new (for us) exit that opens onto the back of the old European-side railway station named Sırkıcı, with its quaint (and expensive) Orient Express café. We have a brief look around, take a few pictures, then look for a more affordable place to eat. Down a couple of side streets and we find a more humble lunch spot. Seated at a little table on the sidewalk we eat a sandwich stuffed with chicken döner—not bad.

After our restorative lunch a short walk brings us to the huge Yeni Cami, the "New Mosque," completed in 1665. Behind this is the Egyptian Spice Bazaar built about the same time. We like to wander through and enjoy the exotic aromas. It is a good place to buy dried hot pepper, which they vacuum pack for you. But we still have plenty on hand from our last visit. We do buy some small ceramic dishes for which Turkey is famous—great gifts if you can get them home in one piece.

Now we are heading back towards the Asian side of Istanbul. But between us and our ferry there is a busy road and a double tramway. Fortunately we are familiar with the underpass. It is packed with people coming and going, and we watch our bags carefully. Here under the flickering fluorescent lights you can purchase anything from expensive jackets to cheap children's toys from the dozens of shops that line the sides of this long underground passage.

Out into the sunlight on the other side and we pass the end of the Galata bridge that crosses the dead-end waterway called the Golden Horn. As usual the bridge is lined with fishermen sitting on their tackle boxes, empty buckets waiting hopefully alongside, hooks dangling in the murky water far below. I'm not sure if I would want to eat those fish. A few hundred yards further and we come to the ferry that will take us back across the Bosporus to the Asian side hub called Kadıköy.

Yes, we are playing tourists today, and we know how to do this on a budget. These ferries are one of the great bargains of Istanbul. The fare costs us less than a dollar each. Tea is even cheaper, though we might splurge and buy a *simit* for another 50 cents. A world class cruise for under five bucks. Through the window, or out on the open deck if the weather is nice and we can bag a seat, we look out on the stately Hagia Sophia church building. What stories she could tell after keeping watch over the strategic Bosporus for so many centuries. Emperor Justinian I, who commissioned the building, would be proud. We admire the magnificent skyline of the city (carefully protected from the encroachment of modern high-rises.) Behind us is the first bridge to connect Europe with Asia, completed in 1973, with an open span of over a kilometre. Bridge number two was completed in 1988. A third bridge, close to the Black Sea, is now under construction.

Nearby we hear the sound of an accordion. A young boy is canvassing the crowd for donations. He is quite good. Further off a man demonstrates a device for getting the most juice from a lemon. I'm sure those lemons are carefully selected. He makes a few sales. I wander down to the lower deck and stand against the rail close to the water. It is impossible to take a bad picture on a day like this. Someone is throwing bread to the gulls and they soar closer and closer. How beautifully these creatures are crafted for flight. The cry of the birds and the smell of the sea come with no extra charge.

The captain expertly jockeys the large vessel alongside the pier as ropes are thrown ashore and men scurry to make us fast. We've just crossed from Europe to Asia. We join the press of commuters rattling over the gangplanks and weave our way out to the street. Kadıköy is the modern site of ancient Chalcedon, home to the Fourth Ecumenical Council of AD 451. But there is very little to see now of ancient history, everything has been built over. Today this is a modern, secular, commercial corner of the larger city of Istanbul.

We walk through some of the areas familiar to us from the time we went to language school here. Nearby is the site of one of the largest weekly street markets in Turkey, but unfortunately this is not market day. Church buildings are rare in this land, but we know of two close by. One is open and we go in for a look around. There is a table displaying free Christian literature. I talk to one of the men watching the door. When I say who we are and where we are from his face softens. Here is a brother. How precious is the family of God that bridges culture and language. That familiar passage comes to mind:

> There is neither Jew nor Greek, [there is neither Turk nor Canadian], there is neither slave nor free, there is no male and female, for you are all one in Christ Jesus (Galatians 3:28).

How hungry we are for this message, especially here, on the edge of the fractured Middle East.

It is time now to find the nearest entrance to the new subway. Soon we are whisked homeward far beneath the troublesome traffic. But we miss the old, above ground commuter train with its ever-changing scenery through the windows. For now that older system is shut down as tracks are being laid for the Istanbul end of the growing high-speed intercity rail network. Best not to stand in the way of progress, especially when it is traveling at 250kms per hour.

Footsore and weary we are glad to get back home and rest. Soon Birkan is home. Politely refusing any help he prepares supper for us all. More talk and tea, with sweet baklava on the side. It is time to check email, then off to bed.

Philemon 4-7 — Recipe For True Spirituality

. . . and I pray that the sharing of your faith may become effective for the full knowledge of every good thing that is in us for the sake of Christ.

. . . .

Heavenly Father, lead me deeper into the reality of this "koinonia of faith."

I'm having trouble understanding just what this means for me.

Is this because it runs counter to my overly independent spirit?

Thank you for the fellowship (koinonia) of your Spirit (2 Cor. 13:14).

And help me to risk koinonia with those believers I still find difficult—former "runaway slaves?"

For have you not drawn even me into koinonia with your very heart?

Amen.

This may be a short, focused, personal letter, but Paul takes time to include his customary thanksgiving and prayer paragraph. Too busy to pray? too busy to give thanks?—not Paul! He is full of thanks for his "grandchildren" in the faith. When I give thanks I am acknowledging that God (not myself) is the primary actor in the events of my life.

Verse six is the transition from thanksgiving to petition. But it turns out to be notoriously difficult to translate. "Full knowledge" is *epignosis*, knowledge that comes not just from learning, but from experience. Paul longs to see Philemon (and the whole church) come to know, from first-hand experience and enjoyment, how rich is the motherlode of blessings given us in Christ.

Though, more precisely, this is "towards" (*eis*) Christ. Thus Paul may be saying that the deeper our understanding and experience of the blessings already "on deposit" within us, the more glory and honour flows to Christ. (Or negatively—Do we, by overlooking, or discounting gospel blessings, shortchange the reputation of Jesus?)

So how do we grow in our appreciation of the Christian gospel? How do we appropriate the rich blessings? How do we move from head knowledge to heart and life knowledge, effectively?

According to Paul's prayer in this verse, it is through the "sharing of our faith." But again, the translation is difficult. Paul does not say, unambiguously, that "talking about our faith" leads to gospel maturity. Nor does he pray they will be faithful in "doing good." Instead he prays for the "*koinonia* of your faith"—the "fellowship," or "communion," or simply "generosity" of your faith. Will Philemon risk extending the *koinonia* of his faith to his runaway slave? Or is his faith too theoretical?

24. Searching for lost sheep

Today Birkan is out of the house early. He leaves his car at home since public transportation is much faster than the crazy rush-hour Istanbul traffic. These days he takes the subway and the ferry, as we did yesterday. His office is on the European side of the city.

Since he has left us with keys to the building and the apartment we are free to come and go as we please. I slip out first to pick up my neatly shortened pants from the tailor. When I try to pay he tells me that Birkan has already paid. Wait till I get hold of that man!

This morning Betty and I plan to walk down to the Sea of Marmara, just fifteen minutes away. The Bosporus does not lead directly to the Mediterranean. First there is this substantial body of water, 280kms by 80kms, that is really Turkey's private inland sea. The Marmara empties through a kind of second Bosporus called the Dardenelles, a narrow strait over 60kms in length and only 1.2kms wide at the narrowest point. From here the water flows into the Aegean Sea before reaching the Mediterranean proper. Just a short ferry ride from shore are the lovely Princes' Islands. If you want a break from the never-ending hustle of Istanbul take a day trip to one or two of these island retreats. Private cars are not allowed, so be prepared to walk, rent a bike, or take a horse-drawn buggy.

Istanbul is over 80kms from end to end. In recent years the city has been cleaning up its extensive waterfront. Industrial areas have been replaced with green space, walkways, and bicycle paths. When we lived here we would often head out for an evening stroll along the Sea of Marmara to watch the sun set over the islands, and wonder about the fishing boats returning home—what treasures were hidden in the hold? And we were never alone along the shoreline. We loved to see couples enjoying a quiet moment together, or energetic young families, full of life, also enjoying the evening air. Optimistic entrepreneurs would set up their little tables and hawk sunflower seeds, or candy floss. Who could resist? One man had a small, hand-cranked merry-go-round that he could wheel from place to place. For a few minutes he would relieve beleaguered mothers of their toddlers (and also relieve them of some spare change).

As Betty and I head out for a walk we meet another former neighbour. With a rare stroke of genius I remember his name. He greets us warmly. How are you doing? How long will you stay? Are your children well? Since we are obviously going out he invites us to his apartment for tea this evening. It least I think this is what he is saying! I will have to ask Birkan to politely check for us.

As we may our way down the steep streets towards the waterfront, a few rain drops begin to fall. We soldier on hoping it won't amount to much. Past familiar shops, the children's park, the internet café, under the pedestrian tunnel at the railway station, through the narrow lanes, then out into the open as we reach the *sahil yolu*, the shore road.

Thankfully the sky has cleared and the sun is out, but the wind is brisk off the water. We are amazed to see a massive new breakwater sheltering the little local harbour. Where did all that material come from?—excavations from the new subway perhaps? It is beautifully constructed. We walk out to the end and back. Some of the little sailboats are for sale. I am tempted, though not Betty. The fishermen's cooperative is still there, and its herd of patient cats. On our return we pass through the crowded local street *pazaar* and buy fruit. It is not hard to slip back into this way of life.

After lunch I head out alone. I am hoping to run into some old street friends. First a trip to the post office to mail some cards. Past my old barber, but he is off today. Then I check out the tea room under the mosque. I spent much time there in the past and got to know the *çaycı*, the tea guy, quite well. I also met with a group of university age guys there, even, unexpectedly, sharing the Gospel with an open Bible—in the very shadow of the mineret, imagine that! But I recognize no one there today. My old friend Ahmed the *çaycı* is gone and a stranger is supervising the large tea urns. I don't sit down for tea, my time is short and I want to move on.

I want to see if my old realtor is still in the same location. This is the chap who found our apartment for us all those years before. We have kept in touch on and off. It's a couple of kilometres away and I am getting my exercise today. I remember the route almost perfectly, just a couple of extra blocks to walk to his little store-front office. And there he is, pleased to see me as always.

When I had stopped by a couple of years earlier he was stooped over a gas ring perched on a small propane tank cooking a simple dish called *menemen* (eggs and tomatoes) for a mid-afternoon snack. I find him doing exactly the same thing today—we laugh over that. Of course I must share the food with him and his colleague. With tea and bread fresh from the bakery it is just what the doctor ordered after my hike.

I discover he is doing very little real estate work these days. His main focus is selling coal. Really? I wonder. Who uses coal in these days of natural gas piped to the door. But he has mostly commercial customers. Though Turkey has a lot of its own coal it is the soft, brown variety. My friend sells high quality coal shipped in from Siberia. Does it pay to ship coal so far? (I also wonder who does the mining up in the notorious region of Siberia.) But my friend talks about how much more BTUs are in a ton of his coal compared to the local stuff. It burns hotter and cleaner, and people buy it.

He asks me if I am still working with the church. In the past I have talked to him about Christ and given him Christian literature. He is open and friendly, but not yet ready to take the leap. Before I head off for home he shows me a recent photo of his two small children. It is good to see him again. Lord remember this man and his family.

On the way back I pass an open plot of land, close to an acre I would guess. It is being used for growing vegetables. At one time this must have been a common sight in the suburbs of Istanbul. But these days almost every square meter of land has a building on it. And the old houses surrounded by their gardens are almost all replaced by apartment buildings. No longer can Istanbul be called "the city of gardens." I stop for a while, leaning on the stone wall, enjoying the tidy rows of lettuce and carrots and more. There isn't a weed in sight.

Philemon 8-22

... that you might have him back forever, no longer as a bondservant but more than a bondservant, as a beloved brother ... in the Lord.

....

Heavenly Father, you are so much more ready to receive the prodigals than we are.

Spur us Lord, to leap over our cultural prejudices, and our social snobbery, and our misogyny.

Our heads know that your grace extends to all people, but our hearts are hard.

Awaken in us the same passion for "three-dimensional unity" in the church that we see here in Paul.

(Not to mention that you have welcomed even me, alien, chief of sinners.)

Praise be to you, O Lord.

Equal In Christ

"There is neither Jew nor Greek, there is neither slave nor free, there is no male and female, for you are all one in Christ Jesus" (Gal. 3:28). What a glorious vision of God's new community. Who could argue against this?

But it's when we get to particulars that our enthusiasm throttles back. You mean we've got to embrace *that* particular ethnic group as equals?! So how did the janitor end up on the board?! And is Philemon supposed to welcome back his run-away slave like a long-lost brother?! Well yes he is, apparently. And Paul pushes every button to compel his friend to do just that.

He pushes the *authority* button—he "subtly" reminds Philemon that, as an apostle of Christ, he could command that he receive Onesimus (8).

He pushes the *pity* button—"I, Paul, an old man and now a prisoner . . ." (9).

He pleads *as a father*—"I appeal to you for my child" (10).

He softens up his friend with *humour*—making a pun on the meaning of the slave's name (11).

He pushes the *guilt* button—he is sending Onesimus back "that your goodness might not be by compulsion but of your own accord" (12-14).

He pushes the *God's will* button—this happened in the providence of God for your benefit (15-16).

He leans on Philemon's *loyalty*—"if you consider me your partner . . ." (17).

He offers (kind of!) to *pay the bill*—if the slave owes anything "charge that to my account" (18-19).

He pleads *neediness*—Do this for me Philemon, "Refresh my heart in Christ" (20).

He announces a *done deal*—I am "confident of your obedience" (21).

He even pushes the *threat* button—By the way, I'll be stopping in for a visit (22).

Why has Paul pulled out all the stops on this organ recital? Surely because the very heart of the Gospel is at stake here. In Christ: *no slave or free!*

25. Last Goodbyes

Back home Birkan soon returns from work. Again he insists on cooking supper. (I guess his mom would kill him if she found out Betty had done the cooking!) We discuss our neighbour's invitation for evening tea. Had I understood him correctly? What time should we go? Years before I had misunderstood a similar invite (from the same gentleman) and it led to some awkwardness. I want to get it right this time. Birkan graciously makes a call and smoothes the waters, and up the stairs we go. It is a good visit and they are pleased we remember them. With the tea comes a sweet pumpkin desert. More Muslim hospitality extended towards these Christian pilgrims. "If you ever need help don't hesitate to get hold of us." In my wallet I still have the slip of paper with their email address and phone number. But we can't stay late. We will be departing early the next morning.

Before six, in fact. Birkan has prepared some food for us to take along. Then he drives us to the ferry terminal ten minutes away. It is not easy to say goodbye, either for him or for us. What can we say? How can we thank him enough? We always seem to be on the receiving end of the relationship. How can we even up the score? We invite him to visit us in Canada. We have a special anniversary coming up next year. How good it would be to host him in our home.

But it is time to go. We purchase our tickets and click through the turnstile into the waiting area, checking twice to make sure we are heading for the right ferry. This is not one of the charming old maidens that gracefully criss-cross the Bosporus. This is a modern, sterile, high-tech, high-speed "cat." We haul our luggage up the gangplank and catch one of the remaining seats by the door. The boat idles out of the harbour, then the captain hits the gas and we skim across the bay to the far end of the European side of the city. Unfortunately we are not allowed to wander round the outside of this boat to enjoy the view and the spray. We have to stay inside during the crossing. Through the fogged up windows we catch a last glimpse of this intriguing city.

For some reason, at the dock in Bakırköy, we are not able to find our connecting bus for the airport. It is likely there somewhere, waiting for the ferry crowd, but we can't find it. There are new buildings sitting on the old bus area. Everything has changed since our last visit. So we hop in a taxi, the price is not that much more. And soon we are safely in the airport, with lots of time to spare. The modern ferries may lack the charm of the traditional boats, but they do provide a fast way of getting from one side of the city to the other. And we have avoided 95% of the rush-hour traffic.

So in this way our modest pilgrimage across Turkey comes to a quiet end. Why do we like this place so much? Yes we enjoy the land, with its deep history, and its rich and varied geography. And we are drawn to the culture of the Middle East, so respectful and civilized and hospitable. But mostly we come because of the particular people we have learned to love. And when you love someone you don't want to lose them. You long to keep connected, not only in this world, but also in the next. May our Lord, in his grace and mercy, use our friendship and our words to bring these dear ones into his Kingdom. Yes, we are weak, but you are strong, O Lord. Bring these dear ones safely into your heavenly harbour. Will this not increase your glory?

By way of a foot note . . . Our trail back to Canada leads through Betty's homeland, the Netherlands, where we will spend some time with her parents and extended family. There (how does this happen?) we meet a Turkish tailor from Konya, called Iconium in the days of the great apostle. Today Konya is a very conservative Muslim city, Paul's visit all those years ago, long forgotten. I also surprise a Turkish butcher by speaking to him in his own language. (He doesn't realize I don't speak Dutch!) He is from Elazığ in the east. They are all homesick. May they become homesick for the meadows of heaven.

Philemon 23-25

... The grace of the Lord Jesus Christ be with your spirit.

....

*Heavenly Father,
we praise you and
worship you, for you are
God Almighty and there is
none like you.*

*How audacious was your
plan, to visit our planet,
and our neighbourhood,
to live, serve, suffer, die,
and rise again—to save
us from the inside out!*

*Praise you, Lord Jesus,
for walking in my shoes,
for learning my language,
for searching me out,
and bringing me home.*

*Glory to you, Holy Spirit,
for your fellowship,
for your encouragement,
your empowering presence.*

*All honour to you,
O Triune God,
for calling us back
to your family table, for
knitting us back together,
for unshattering my heart.*

Amen, and Amen.

Amazing Grace

It is the closing greetings that tie this letter so closely to Paul's letter to the church in Colossae. The same five people are with Paul in both. The list includes Luke and Mark, who together with Paul, wrote most of the New Testament, plus Epaphras, the founding father of the church in Colossae. No pressure Philemon, but these men too, are watching to see how you welcome Onesimus!

So we imagine Tychicus setting out to deliver Paul's letter to the church in Colossae. And alongside him Onesimus clutching Paul's passionate plea to Philemon (Col. 4:7f.) His whole future, perhaps even his very life, hangs on Philemon's response. And we can imagine the prodigal slave alternating between faith and anxiety, the closer he gets.

To visit Colossae today is to visit a pile of rubble, a city very dead. Yet remarkably this little letter to the Colossian slave-owner is still very much alive. As it turned out, Philemon did not just tear it up and toss it angrily in the fire. Surely we have this letter today because he did understand and accept Paul's penned sermon. *Yes, you are right Paul, Onesimus is now my brother.*

In a curious historical footnote, a letter has been preserved, written by Ignatius, Bishop of Antioch, as he was being taken in chains to his martyrdom in Rome. In this letter, written to the church in Ephesus, he refers to their "excellent Bishop, Onesimus . . . a man of inexpressible love."

We cannot be sure this is the same person, but how fitting for this man, once an "unprofitable" slave (11), to be so transformed by Jesus as to rise to such prominence in the most important city of the region. On the wall of his office, framed for all to see, hangs the original copy of his emancipation papers, signed by Paul himself!

Either way, the slave economy of Rome could not hold out against this Gospel. Untold Philemons were indeed filled with the grace of our Lord, and received their converted slaves as brothers.

www.ingramcontent.com/pod-product-compliance
Lightning Source LLC
Chambersburg PA
CBHW020544030426
42337CB00013B/975